– My Bod

Zhang Xianliang, born in 1936, is the author of the internationally acclaimed *Half of Man is Woman, Getting Used to Dying* and *Grass Soup*. He is currently working on a family biography that covers the last century of Chinese history. He lives in Ningxia, western China.

Martha Avery is currently based in Ulaanbaatar, where she is Director of the Publishing Program of the Soros Foundation in Mongolia. She continues to translate the work of Zhang Xianliang; her own most recent book is *Women of Mongolia*.

by the same author

Half of Man is Woman
Getting Used to Dying
*Gra** Soup**

*available in Minerva

Zhang Xianliang

MY BODHI TREE

Translated from the Chinese by
MARTHA AVERY

Minerva

A Minerva Paperback
MY BODHI TREE

First published in Great Britain in 1996
by Martin Secker & Warburg Ltd
This Minerva edition published in 1997

Random House UK Limited
20 Vauxhall Bridge Road, London SW1V 2SA

Random House Australia (Pty) Limited
20 Alfred Street, Milsons Point, Sydney
New South Wales 2061, Australia

Random House New Zealand Limited
18 Poland Road, Glenfield, Auckland 10, New Zealand

Random House South Africa (Pty) Limited
Endulini, 5a Jubilee Road, Parktown 2193, South Africa

Random House UK Limited Reg. No. 954009

Originally published in Chinese in 1994 as *Wode Bodi Shu*
by Beijing Zuojia Chubanshe

Copyright © 1994 by Zhang Xianliang
Translation and introduction copyright © 1996 by Martha Avery
The author and translator have asserted their moral rights

A CIP catalogue record for this title is available from the British Library
ISBN 0 7493 8605 3

Phototypeset in Palatino by Intype London Ltd
Printed and bound in Great Britain
by Cox & Wyman Ltd, Reading, Berkshire

Introduction

The years 1960–62 are called the 'three years of natural disaster' in China. Weather was blamed for poor harvests and lack of food. In fact the problems stemmed from disruption of the agrarian economy due to policies dictated by Mao Zedong at the time of the Great Leap Forward (1958).

During this three-year period, an estimated thirty million people died of starvation in China. Increasing numbers of political prisoners were also consigned to labour camps. The lunacy of national policies extended to local counties and villages, and decided the fate of individuals throughout the country.

This book annotates a diary that was kept by the author in 1960. It was written in a labour reform camp where one-third of the several thousand inmates died. The author survived, and he considers the experience to have been his 'bodhi tree', in Buddhist terms, the place of his enlightenment.*

The book is a record of actual events, but it is also a call to the world to learn from the past. Witness to starvation, to cannibalism, to people betraying each other in order to survive, the author examines the psychology that allowed this disaster to happen. In the process he also details the psychology of survival. Among the lessons that emerge from the book is the recognition that personal fortitude is based on self-

---

* Shakyamuni, the historical Buddha, achieved enlightenment while meditating under a bodhi tree.

esteem, and self-esteem is impossible when there is unquestioning acceptance of outside authority.

Another lesson is the tenacity of the human spirit. Zhang's message is ultimately one of hope: he believes in, and he writes for, the future.

Martha Avery

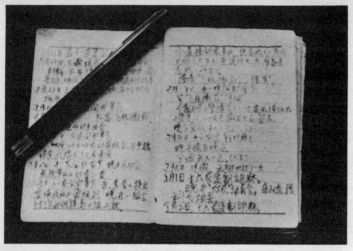

The original diary (July 1960–March 1961).

Taken just before I was sent (for the first time) to labour reform camp after being declared a rightist in 1958.

Taken just before I was sent to prison in 1970, during the One-Blow-Three-Counters Movement, after release in 1969 from my second stint in labour reform.

Note: The photographs of Zhang Xianliang were taken by government authorities in charge of the camp and the prison.

Evening had fallen by the time I crawled up the canal bank to have a look. We had been ordered to cut grass overtime, so we worked till it was late. It was too dark to see much, but I could smell the odour – the fleeting fragrance, faint and sweet, of raw blood. I can still smell it today. Sometimes it's as though it is being wafted from a distant place, sometimes it is right under my nose.

Excerpted from the end of *Grass Soup*, which covers the first part of Zhang Xianliang's labour-camp diary. *My Bodhi Tree* completes the annotations of the diary.

我的菩提樹

1960

1 September

Worked at the north pigpen, filling in holes. Got three *mao**
of tobacco from Su Xiaosu in the morning, split it up and
gave one mao's worth to Ding Haijie. Tobacco extremely
precious now. People with money can still buy things in the
camp; some with money don't know how to do this, others
manage to get things without any money.

According to Liu Xueru's son, people in communes in
Hebei** are as emaciated and weak as we are. Everyone's
in the same shape but we're not allowed to say it.

Pigs are pitifully thin, but the pen is sturdy. Methods of
pig-raising terribly unscientific. Our farm shouldn't be like
this. Hauled the cart for a day, exhausted. Near quitting time
Chen and Heh nearly came to blows over who had to pull
it. I could see there would be trouble and pulled it home
myself.

Rollcall was called this evening before I'd finished eating.
Troop Leader Sun gave a report, said a lot of new people had
come in, warned us not to go spreading negative attitudes
among them.

---

* A mao is one-tenth of a yuan, or approximately ten pence. (All
footnotes are the translator's – M.A.)
** The province surrounding Beijing.

As I read this diary the past wells up again, surging toward me counter to the passage of time. Parts of my life spit back at me like frozen spray on the wave of history, but by now the chapters are out of sequence. I lose my sense of balance – assaulted by events from the past, slipping on the ridge between past and future, I am uncertain which way to allow my sweaty body to slide. Unimaginable depths lie on either side.

Copying out the original text of the diary, line by line, I feel as though each individual word should be explained. It is increasingly clear that the point of contact between past and future lies with my immediate now-ness, with this very moment, this second. But with irre-futable decisiveness the passage of time continues to split what will be from what has gone. As it does, not only does it have the potential to rip me in two – it has the power to shred the world.

Were it not for the future I would not put myself through this again. But I feel a responsibility to piece together the disjointed events of that period, to restore the complete picture. I owe this to the being that both allowed me to survive and endowed me with the capacity to remember and record. There must have been a reason to be selected from among the tens of millions who died – so that I am now fortunately walking, sitting, living, sleeping on top of this Earth rather than buried beneath it.

I have written a number of novels and yet I am help-less against this tumult of memories. They cannot be dealt with, conquered by, writing skills of which we authors so often speak. Techniques that I have honed and practised – character portrayal, plot development, descriptive background – lose their meaning here. They are crippled by the rawness of such intense source material. Real life cannot be accommodated within the framework of the written word.

After looking over the original text of the diary and what I wrote in *Grass Soup*,* I realize that my explanations are incomplete. It would be impossible to clarify, one by one, things that the contemporary reader finds hard to comprehend. And yet I must address them and do so clearly, for everything that is unclear to mankind must be played out again. What I write about is called 'history' even though the air around us still carries in its freshness the stench of rotting corpses.

It would be pleasant to develop amnesia, as others do, and become involved in the flow of both happiness and senseless sorrow in the world. History, after all, will take care of itself. Without stopping to fret about a people who lost their reason, it may throw garlands or it may fling sewage, but it will silently move on. The venerable being or force of nature that bestowed life and intelligence on me will not, however, allow me to stay silent. She comes to me like a recurring nightmare, like an inner compulsion; she becomes an encircling wall that cuts me off from the rest of mankind. Any happiness I have in this world today comes from the past. When my hand is about to touch the shadow of the past, when my eyes can see rays of light that have disap-

* *Grass Soup* covers the first half of the diary; *My Bodhi Tree* covers the second half.

4

peared, when my nose can smell the stink or the fragrance from the depths of time, I find rest.

I just saw that rough old thin-planked casket again. We called it a casket but it was really only a rectangular box made of boards nailed together. The poplar, recently chopped down, then sawn and planed into nearly translucent thin boards, gave off the wet smell of freshly cut timber. Its exposed growth rings revealed a dragon-in-clouds, head showing, tail hidden. The casket sat before the door of the carpenter's shed, outside the big yard of the labour camp. Still covered by sawdust and shavings, it looked long and sleek, a well-trained horse waiting for its master. He would soon be riding it down that long road to another world.

Our way to the north pigpen went by the carpenter's shed with this proud casket. Looking in, I had the feeling that the dead man inside was looking out, surveying the sky of a world he had known, a world that brought so many troubles to men.

The convicts spoke in tones of admiration and envy.

'Dogshitter even managed to get hold of a casket!'

'No wonder he decided to commit suicide. He had this whole thing planned long ago!'

'Won't be so bad if I can have a longevity-casket* like that – I don't care what you say, it's still a kind of home.'

'Forget it. It'll just be harder for the dogs to drag you out to gnaw on, that's all.'

It was true that the casket did not speak, had no way to express itself, yet it seemed to emanate a self-satisfied air. It seemed so clean, so fresh, so cool. It was even ventilated, and far more comfortable than the thirty-to-

---

* Casket prepared before one's death, for perpetual residence.

fifty-centimetre-wide dirty bunks we slept on each night. It was so enticing that we all felt like crawling in for a nap.

Not one of us spent a moment pondering the man's suicide or drawing any lessons from it. I personally felt nothing but a little disappointment about the event. I would have liked to see his wife and daughter again. They weren't around the casket and were nowhere to be seen at Farm Headquarters – a free convict said that the woman collapsed after the suicide and the Old Commissar, concerned about her, let her recuperate in the camp's infirmary.

In those days, not only prisoners and convicts but citizens in general knew what they should think and what they had better not think. We understood, of course, what not to say, but we even knew what to avoid feeling. Our ways of thinking and feeling were already so reformed that it suited the leaders' needs exactly. Unthinkable thoughts and emotions were like petty thieves: as soon as they appeared in our minds we found them out and swiftly expelled them. The fact that a man had ended his life in such a terrible way did not raise the slightest ripple of concern among us. Everything was the same. Labour reform continued as usual.

Ma Weixiao also had a visit from a country relative on the same day. We learned this only after we had gone home that night, since the leaders had not let Ma's relatives come out to the fields.

By the time we got back to the big yard, marching under stars that were already brilliant, I saw these relatives guarding a pile of things as they squatted by the gate. They were unmistakable: two old Muslim men wearing small white hats on their heads. I was as happy

6

as Ma was at seeing them, and forgot what I had seen that afternoon. Before the Troop Leader came to notify Ma that he could receive guests, I quickly took a sweet potato from my chest and tucked it in my bedding, mud and all. Then I opened a seam of my cotton-padded mattress and took a half-*jin** grain coupon from a secret place hidden in the corner. I gave Ma this half-jin coupon to get a Guest Meal.

Ma Weixiao did not stoop to getting Guest Meals for himself when a relative came to visit. He had better things to eat. He generously agreed to help me out. When he returned to the Number** later that evening he put his own large package of food down and then silently stuffed two deep-brown steamed millet buns in my hands.

With sweet potatoes already stashed, I was now instantly wealthy. Who would have thought that I should be so very fortunate, so replete, when someone else, namely the suicide's wife, was in such pain? The world is truly abundant in its diversity. Going to the north pigpen the next day I saw the casket but was as insensitive as everyone else. After a good meal, yesterday's horror did not seem particularly horrifying.

On the way to work the millet buns and raw sweet potatoes sloshed around inside me, making my shrivelled stomach produce too much acid. I was fixated on the very real possibility that I might get diarrhoea. 'Even a good man fears three runny shits in a row,' convicts often said. If I was unlucky and got dysentery I would

* A jin is equivalent to about half a kilogram.
** General name for the barracks in a camp, so called because each building had a number.

7

probably not recover. And if I died, I would not be so fortunate as to enjoy this kind of casket, for except for special occasions that high-class treatment was long gone. I would simply have died at the wrong time.

The convicts had reason to envy this dead ghost his coffin. In 1958, the labour reform authorities made no distinction among the kinds of people pressed into the camps. Day and night, wave upon wave of people washed in. That was at the time of the so-called Great Leap Forward, and when a convict died he was still given a casket like this one parked by the shed. In those days it was generally carried suspended from two carrying poles, hoisted by four free convicts.*

Later, the supply of wood could not keep up with demand. The tall beautiful poplars that had grown naturally in the area, many decades old, were all cut down to the ground. It was painful to see. After that, dead convicts had to make do with a woven reed mat rolled around them. This would be dragged out of the big yard, either sideways or lengthwise. Even reed mats required a lot of labour, however, and reed mats could be used as building material for the living, to block the wind and rain. They soon became too important to use as packing material for dead people. By the time food was scarce, reed mats were also scarce, so the disposition of corpses had also arrived at a 'lowered standard'.**

---

* A 'free convict' was one who had served his sentence and nominally been released, but who still worked inside the camp for a living. These men enjoyed more freedom than regular convicts.
** Refers to the lowered amount of rationed food – instead of grain, people were asked by the government to eat more 'gourds and vegetables'.

The dead had to share the inconvenience and take to the road completely naked.

'Completely naked' is no exaggeration. At the end of their lives, dead convicts were disposed of without a single stitch of clothing – they went to their graves exactly as they were when they emerged from their mothers' wombs. If they died when the earth had not yet frozen hard they were lucky – the dirt that covered them could be a little thicker. If they happened to die in the freezing cold winter they were doubly cursed. A shovel would sprinkle a smattering of dirt over them and they would be considered 'buried'.

The labour reform camp couldn't afford the cost of reed mats, but the authorities had not yet reached the mean stage of stripping off a convict's clothes. The people handling the burial of convicts were not camp officials but free convicts. Every dead convict's burial was, for them, an opportunity for enrichment.

In pairs, or with four people working together, depending on how many corpses were to be buried, they would take the dead to the graveyard either in small carts or large horsewagons. The graveyard was a stretch of alkaline wasteland to the north of the Main Headquarters' Canal Sixteen. Once there, the free convicts would sit down and rest. When they felt they had rested sufficiently, they would start to dig a pit. A spot would be chosen where there was already a natural declivity in the land, to save work. Just one pit would be prepared, no matter how many dead were to be buried. It would be larger or smaller depending on whether there were lots of corpses or just a few. What free convicts liked best was a large collective burial.

When the pit was dug, they would start to strip the

9

clothes off the corpses. One by one they would unclothe them as though preparing to give them a bath – but when they had one stripped naked, they wouldn't put him in a bathtub, they would just toss him into the pit. If someone had been a smoker, there were sure to be secret pockets in his clothes for hiding old cigarette butts. The free convicts would carefully shake out the treasure, then split up the dead man's inheritance into equal shares. The original owner had no option but to lie there on the ground, shameless in his nakedness. Only when they had rolled his remaining tobacco in bits of paper and smoked it was he allowed to take his final definitive leave from his own patch of sky.

The reason I am so clear about these details – how free convicts would shake cigarette butts from dead men's pockets and smoke them – is that I knew a particular free convict who worked this trade. After he was released he returned to his home country where he would gather friends together and relate with great vigour and specificity stories about the droves of people who died in the camps. Because of this, when the Socialist Education Movement began, he was slapped with the crime of fabricating counter-revolutionary rumours and sent in once again for labour reform. When I met up with him in my second stint of labour reform, he still took delight in narrating details about burying dead people in 1960, as though there had been little else in his life worth remembering. According to him, his hands had buried hundreds of people. You could tell from his descriptions that he knew better than any gynaecologist the many types and categories of vulva. He often used his fist to indicate the Venus mound of the female sex: the cracks between his fingers would be the labia. He would wriggle the fingers around to show different shapes and sizes, educating convicts in this important field of expertise.

I personally knew something about burying people. One time, I found myself violently angry with him as a result.

'You dogshitters stripped the bodies even before you dragged them to their final resting place,' I yelled at him. 'Don't you motherfuckers have any conscience at all?!'

He said nothing, just stared hard at me, then snickered. 'How do you know?' he asked. 'Eh, how do you know?'

Even today I don't understand why death has stayed so close to me. Theoretically one can say that life is the same as death, in the sense that both stem from the same great void.* In the concrete world of phenomena, however, life and death are undeniably different. On my own body, abstract philosophy often manifests itself in an extremely concrete way. Just as I feel my physical being as the link between past and future, I often feel that abstract and concrete are united in my person. I feel this most strongly in my fingers. I often stop to look at them as I write this book. Slowly, I begin to feel the slight coolness of death coming from my fingertips. My fingers have touched death, the concrete reality of a person's cold flesh, countless times. I was not a forensic doctor or some kind of aide at a funeral parlour – at that time I was a poet and the dead were not supposed to be part of my profession.

By the time I did labour reform the second time, I was

* A Buddhist belief.

fairly tough. I was also by then a so-called 'second-time-returned-to-the-palace' convict, a 'big-small rightist', and an 'old-brand rightist'. In short, I was an old hand. Since that made me more highly regarded by the leaders, I'd been given the additional title of Big Team Leader – I was a sort of king among convicts. As a result, I did not condescend to answer this man who so loved to bury women. I stood up when he asked me how I knew and merely slapped his face. I added a few kicks to his stomach. 'Teach you to love looking at cunt! Teach you to love looking at cunt!' I kicked until he was curled up in a ball and rolling on the ground.

After the rage, I slowly calmed down. Naturally, I am even calmer today. I look silently at my fingers, turning them over and over, and the feeling of the past rises from within them like smoke curling from five thin columns. The sensation now carries with it a sense of abundance, a sense that I have the power to see the actual boundary between life and death.

When I say death, I don't mean the one, two, three, four . . . who died beside me in the early days. I mean the multitude of dead who, when I was most unprepared for it and indeed just beginning to feel new hope, suddenly broke into my sense of touch and awareness.

In the early spring of 1960, that is to say five months before I started writing this diary, the weather was extremely cold. Because they were hungry, people's sense of being cold was much more acute than one would have expected from the actual temperature. From morning to night there was never a moment that one felt warm. Often one's entire body would be shaking. At night one would curl up tightly in the bedding and then go to work the next morning without ever having felt warm – it seemed colder inside the thin blanket than it was outside.

Under these circumstances, fire became a primary necessity. When the eighteen men in our Group returned home, we were like a brood of piglets struggling to get close to our mother's teats, all fighting to crowd up to a half-dead stove. Thirty-six hands would obscure the mouth of the stove, everyone trying to get his hands the closest. One hand on top first, then on the bottom, eighteen pairs of hands danced in a choreographed movement.

The labour reform troop dispensed a mere fifteen jin of 'mud charcoal' to each Number per month. Mud charcoal was a revolutionary creation born of the time of the Great Leap Forward. The reason it had never been seen in history before was that even primitive man in his cave had never dreamed of it as a source of warmth. It was simply the rotted roots and stems of reeds that came from the frozen bottom of the swamp. It came in large chunks, black and sooty, so that the exterior did indeed look very much like a proper piece of coal. And it could be made to burn. If you used quantities of dry branches to get it lit, it would finally glow dull red and give us a sense of 'fire'.

But, fifteen jin of this material was quite insufficient for our needs. So we came up with a second source of warmth, namely the bits of charcoal that fell through the bottom of the stove grate in the kitchen. Although these had already been burned once, they were made of true coal, what people in Beijing called coal-lumps or what people in the north-west more descriptively called charcoal knobs. The poor people of the old society relied on these as the main source of fuel in their homes.

There were many hundreds of convicts, several dozen Numbers ... yet there were only four cooking stoves. The coal bits that fell from the grates were not enough for all of us, and as usual the race went to the swiftest. Every day each group* would send a man to the kitchen to grab these coal bits. He had to get out of bed before anyone else, shoulder his back-basket before the morning star had risen, and go and wait near the stove grate of the big kitchen. When the cooks had finished cooking and were getting ready to put out the fire, the little bits of charcoal would come rattling down. Never mind that the stove was still burning crimson and belching smoke – the appointed man would leap forward and rake in coals as though his life depended on it. And never mind about burning your hands. Hands were like frozen blocks of ice. Being burned and being full were two sensations I did not experience for many years.

Every half month it was my turn. I enjoyed this job. You had to get out of bed early, but squatting below the stove of the big kitchen was far warmer than staying all balled up in an ice-cold bed. Coughing and yawning, I would listen drowsily to the other men gossiping, passing along all kinds of news: where to find something to eat, who desperately needed to trade something, the latest method of cooking sweet potatoes, how to get the cabbage you'd stolen during the day home to your Number, whose old lady was starting divorce proceedings against him, who had died, etc. The sounds all

---

* A group was composed of around twenty men, and was headed by a Group Leader, a man selected by the camp authorities from among the convicts.

seemed to reverberate in a dream, from whose depths wafted the occasional fragrance of the cook's thin gruel.

In that trance-like reverie, between dreaming and not-dreaming, the two sharply different worlds of life and death seemed to merge.

One day it was again my turn to be on duty. I crawled out of bed, rubbed my eyes, picked up the back-basket and headed for the big kitchen. Up to that moment I still believed I was sleeping. I saw the light from the stove's fire ahead as nothing more substantial than the comfort of a dream. The moon was still suspended in the sky like a frozen orb, its icicle rays of light unusually brilliant. Suddenly, a vision of two large carts laden with wicker baskets brought me sharply awake. Their absolute reality assaulted my senses. They were parked just outside the gate of the big yard, which for some reason had been left open. A large piece of canvas covered the baskets piled inside, and these had clearly been packed to the brim.

Now, what sort of thing would farm carts be piled full of? Naturally things that farms produced! And what sort of thing was that? Why it would be vegetables or grain, that sort of thing! My stomach began to rumble violently in anticipation and my mouth flowed with saliva.

The sluggish men on duty from the other groups had not yet noticed. They were still drawn up around the foot of the stove. I took advantage of their inattentiveness to slip like a ghost's shadow out of the gate. I brought my back-basket with me, of course, to load up what I was going to steal. I thought happily of how I would go home today with a full haul.

The wicker baskets had been packed so full that they

were bulging like balls. I stepped on the axle of one large cart and, lifting a corner of the canvas with one hand, stretched my other arm and hand inside.

Damn! Seemed to be cabbages, but also might be sweet potatoes! Just that the cabbage heads seemed too big. I'd never known such large cabbages or potatoes before, and each one seemed to be pressing hard against the next. I felt here and there, top to bottom, and yet couldn't get to the two ends of what was inside. 'Can't be choosy when you're stealing things,' I told myself, 'dither over this or that. Grab hold and pull!' I seized something and pulled upward with all my might. I pulled to the left, I pulled to the right. No matter what, I was going to get this thing out.

I finally managed to extricate an item from the large pile. An arm, exactly like mine, came swinging violently out of the canvas.

It glowed with a dull greenish white in the moonlight, just like frozen cabbage. The hand was curled, the five fingers were slightly separated in the elegant attitude of playing a violin. The arm was already frozen stiff, without the slightest feel of flesh about it. Small wonder I had not realized earlier that the cart was packed with human beings.

I sank to the ground, numb with shock. Fortunately I had long since had some experience with the dead, so this little bunch of them was not completely destabilizing. I slumped beneath the axle of the cart for a while, fright gradually transforming itself into disappointment. Perversely, I began to feel that these dead people were messing around with me, making me lose a superb chance to steal some food. I felt a kind of hatred towards them.

I finally came to as the clang of cooking issued from the direction of the big kitchen. I climbed up, shouldered my back-basket and headed for the stove where all the good charcoal lumps had long ago been swept up by others. Collecting a few useless cinders, I went on home. Our head of the household, the Little Group Leader, was already up and the small oil lamp was lit. The Group Leader yawned as he swung my basket off to examine my contribution.

'You bastard!' he swore. 'You're good for nothing but burning coal! You don't know how to get it! Look at what you've picked up. You think these have anything left in them?!'

Other convicts added fuel to the flames. 'Fine him! Fine him a day of fuel! No fire for him today!'

The criminal convicts* were much kinder. One got me off the hook by saying, 'Group Leader, I've got an idea. Every day we waste a lot of energy, running out before it's light to get these charcoal knobs. It would be much better for us to go around to other groups and steal their mud coal!'

After that we were busy lining up and getting our food, then busy taking it back and eating it. By the time I had finished drinking my thin gruel I had calmed down somewhat. Only then did I recall the unanticipated feeling of grabbing hold of dead people.

Men or women, they were all completely naked. Some of the skin had been slippery, like Chinese cabbage, some had been rough, rather like sweet potatoes. They were jumbled together, their limbs intertwined. Whether

* Men convicted of real crimes, not political prisoners. These men were generally not intellectuals.

they had come originally from the five lakes or the four oceans, in the end they had bonded together here in an intimate mass of bodies.

Since my thoughts were on food when I touched them, the sensation was thereafter closely associated with things to eat. From that time on I have not been able to look at cooked meat hanging in a store. I cannot hold an uncooked chicken or duck leg that has been de-feathered after slaughter. If I see or touch this kind of thing my stomach turns and I vomit bile. In the labour camps there was none of this sort of food, of course, and so the psychosis took time to show itself. Two decades later, with the markets prosperous and well stocked, this strange reaction has become pronounced to the point that I am basically a vegetarian.

Naturally, I couldn't tell the other convicts what I had just seen. I've already noted that we had already been reformed to the point that we knew exactly what could be said and what could not be said. If I mentioned this event, a light punishment might call for self-examination. A heavier punishment would be 'elevation in rank', that is, in severity of crime and length of stay in the camp. The memory of the bodies could only be stashed away inside me, but they never rotted away there, and they have haunted me for a lifetime.

Those stories from that free convict of burying women came later. By then, convicts didn't give a damn about how someone who might have been sleeping next to them was disposed of. Another man's corpse was not your property. You couldn't go around worrying about how it was wrapped, how it was transported, and to where. If someone in your group died, he died. You went to work as usual, came back from work as usual, and if as you went to work you saw his corpse lying out on display, publicly defying the system by not going to the fields, you might even feel a tinge of envy. When you came home the corpse would be gone – do you think you would ask about whether it was carried out or dragged out, whether it was stripped of its clothes or left with some on? If the man died during the night you would just be happy to get an extra one-seventeenth of breakfast. If he died in the morning, you would get one-seventeenth more for lunch; if he died in the afternoon you might get the extra portion in the evening.

Even if you knew that some friend of yours had been stripped like a newborn babe when he died, it was hard to criticize the free convict in charge of the burial. That free convict who carried out the study of Yin* corpses defended himself with: 'What a shame to have clothes rot there in the ground, or just be torn to shreds by dogs!' It was true. If you were so poor that your eyes glowed as red as burning coals, you too would feel that it was a waste to let clothes rot for nothing.

That same spring, shortly after I pawed through the pile of corpses, a rumour started among the convicts to the effect that a high-ranking convict, a being-looked-after convict, had secretly written a letter to the Central Politburo of the Party.** He had a visiting relative carry it out of the camp for him, to make sure it was sent. In the letter he noted that large numbers of convicts were dying in the labour camps.

Now when we went to and from work each day, whenever we saw a stranger, we would assume he was

---

* Female, as opposed to the male principle, or Yang.
** 'Central' for short, as below.

sent from Central. This hope and expectation lasted for more than half a year, but no strange cadre seemed to fit the role. On 1 September, however, the authorities suddenly had us go to the infirmary for a collective health checkup. This uncommon event is mentioned in the diary entries.

We convicts lined up by groups in front of the infirmary, which was in the big yard of the camp. An earthen-clod building, this was no different from the Numbers we lived in except that a large red cross was painted on its rickety wooden door. Those who liked to pretend to be a Sick Number, including me, would generally stroll by here every day. Even today, a red cross on a building holds a seductive appeal, like a tourist attraction. Back then the purpose of coming here was not to be cured. Everyone knew that the only medicines on earth that could cure our ills were rice and steamed buns. Besides, the doctors could only dispense a few 'three-bromide' pills and 'ferrous sulphuric acid' that neither cured any-thing nor filled the stomach.

Our real purpose in coming to the infirmary was to have the doctor grant 'full-rest' or 'half-rest' status. He would not hand a slip directly to the convict, but would write the name of the person allowed to be sick on a separate form. The next day, when the Troop Leader took rollcall before work, he would call out the names indicated on the doctor's list and let them stay home. Full rest was nearly the same as the status of those much-envied dead people – you could blatantly stay put on your bunk-bed and sleep, waiting for the two men beside you to leave so that your 'patch of earth and sky' was no longer limited to thirty centimetres.

Half rest would mean you still had to put in the

appearance of going to work, but after one or two hours you could knock off and the rest of the time would be yours. Naturally, with a little more inside you than a dead person, you could wander in the yard, go from Number to Number, inquire where there might be something to eat or where you could trade a few things. If you still had stolen cabbages or potatoes that you had hidden away, now was when you could cook them slowly and enjoy them.

Earthen clods littered the yard – with three of these you could make a little cooking hearth. If you saw someone tearing down part of the wall that surrounded us, he was not trying to escape, just trying to get a better clod for his stove. Almost every convict had his own hearth.

But on the afternoon of 1 September, all of the convicts, whether they were sick or not, were gathered by groups before the red cross. They whispered to one another, debating the rumour that had started half a year earlier. Surely this unprecedented physical examination had been caused by that letter that had managed to get through the net. Central wanted to know if the situation was truly that serious.

'Food's bound to get better now. If not, a lot more of us are going to be dead!'

'Examination! Balls! All they've got to do is use their eyes! See how we're nothing but racks of bones!'

'Lowered standard: that's like scratching your rear-end with a live hand grenade. If you don't give a man enough to eat, you're basically saying you don't give a damn about whether or not he stays alive.'

The lid was kept on the muttered remarks so long as we had no physical exam at all. Once an exam was held, counter-revolutionary talk erupted all over. Yet not one of those who dared to say these things was an intellectual over thirty. Older intellectuals stood carefully in line, arms folded, shoulders drooping, silently doing their best to indicate that they were so weak that a breath of wind might knock them over. At the same time, their faces were well composed in an expression of supreme gratitude to Central. No matter what age or type of convict, everyone was hoping to receive a verdict of 'grave symptoms'. Nobody cared what the actual illness might be. Cancer could hardly scare men on the verge of death. First it was necessary to let Central know the results of not getting enough rations, so that they would immediately issue more grain. The idea was to eat at least one full meal, and then worry about living or dying.

But the physical examination was a great disappointment. As noted in my diary, 'it was no more than weighing and measuring height'. It was even more superficial than a normal exam – they didn't even touch a stethoscope to our chests. One convict-doctor measured height, another took care of weight, while a third made notes in a booklet. This assembly-line process meant that as soon as a convict entered the flow he was hustled through and re-emerged in seconds. Within one afternoon they had examined the bodies of several hundred convicts.

My height was 1.78 metres, my gross weight 47 kilograms. Without the clothes, shoes and pants I had on that were covered with mud, my net weight was 44 kilograms.

When convicts are dissatisfied they begin to complain.

'Motherfucker! This is messing around with Central. Deceiving them, pure and simple.'

'Plus you don't know what that last dogshitter was writing in his book. Hard telling – he might have been writing down that you were fat as a pig!'

'Tell that cadre to write another letter to Chairman Mao, exposing how they're trying to trick him!'

Ma Weixiao approached me as everyone left the area. From the look in his deep-set mystical eyes I could tell that he was unable to hold back some kind of 'counter-revolutionary thesis'. I was both anxious about hearing something I knew I shouldn't and interested to know what it might be. Nobody was paying attention, and I leaned over to hear what he had to say.

'Those idiots haven't a clue. Chairman Mao wants to be deceived by those below him!'

'Chairman Mao wants to be deceived?' Stupefied, I repeated this back as I stared at him. But he turned and floated out of the crowd of convicts, going to eat his own good things in his Number. I was left gazing at his erect figure as he walked away.

This one sentence, this counter-revolutionary thesis, plagued me for years. At times I considered it nonsense, at other times it clearly seemed to be true. An article I read later described the ideal qualities of a leader, what a leader should prepare himself to be, and this helped my understanding. An intelligent leader not only has to excel at deceiving others, when the need arises he must also allow others to deceive him – in the interests of higher goals. If this were not so, how could a man born of peasants, who had personally planted crops in the field, believe in all innocence that one *mou* of land could produce one hundred and sixty thousand jin of rice?

23

How else could he institute a large-scale state purchasing programme throughout the country so that in the end it was necessary for eight hundred million Chinese to try to survive on half their normal food?

The reality of what happened later proved that this particular leader was indeed very good at pretending to believe that certain impossible things were true.

10 September

Still the same work as yesterday. At the fields, Heh Deng
started a fight with Liu Xueru over how to allocate workload.
Heh also disagreed with Chen Lin. Heh's negativity severe
lately. Today he was gong to write a report resigning his Group
Leader status. In order not to make things hard for both sides,
I again stepped forward to haul the cart.

Not allowed to rest at noon. Zheng lectured us. Our group
was criticized. Liu Xueru's practice of selling salt was
brought up without mentioning names. Zhou was labelled a
bad egg. Without any rest, Feng Guozuo said that what we
were doing was exhaustion reform, not labour reform.

Afternoon Liu Xueru, Zhou, Liu Fengxiang reported one
by one to Troop Leader Zheng. Seems they all have a bellyful
of grievances.

Today I put on new clothes and new shoes. Who was I
saving them for, anyway? Still timid and nervous when I go
to get food, need to control it.

New labour reform convicts arrived. The weather is already
cold, cotton-padded shirt and pants still not issued. Very
worried.

In evening we judged who was to get awards for
meritorious service, who was to receive praise, etc. Everyone
snickering, not serious in the slightest.

11 September

Chest hurt last night, not able to sleep well. Went to Farm
Thirteen's pigpen again today. Morning asked Chen Lin to
let me rest; he wouldn't allow it, but I lay down beside the
pigs for half an hour.

At break Chen Lin called a meeting, turns out Zhou again
stole watermelons, sunflower seeds, sweet potatoes. Zhou
did a self-examination, but also ate up everything he'd stolen.
'Balls!' Zhou said. 'Complains about our eating a few
sunflower seeds, but Chen Lin himself is getting double meals
and we're not supposed to notice when he takes a watermelon!'

Heh Deng made a small iron stove in one morning, put his
entire soul into it, was discovered by a pigpen convict who
reported to Troop Leader Zheng. Heh cursed out the man
who reported on him.

Troop Leader Zheng found Zhou and talked for a long

time. They were not happy when they parted. According to Zhou, Zheng got angry at him because he asked Zheng why some people are fat while others are so thin.

Afternoon Chen Lin called rollcall before the whole troop, said there were a lot of people talking nonsense in front of newly arrived convicts, spreading negative attitudes. Back in the Number, I saw that our group had been allocated two new convicts, both cadres from Y City's Geomorphology Department. Heh received them without enthusiasm. First thing he said was, 'Water's scarce. Can't let anyone drink as much as he wants. Have to ration it!'

I don't know why, but the latter part of the diary is written in much more detail. As the days go by, it appears that life in the camps was not so bad as my current nightmares would indicate. Freedom can exist anywhere. So long as you are crafty enough, slippery enough and cynical enough about the world, and sufficiently cold and disengaged when you are tricked and cheated, then you will always have an adequate measure of it. On the other hand, if you conscientiously abide by society's rules of conduct even though society does not regard you or treat you as human, then you will not survive for long.

Free markets were extremely lively in labour reform camps. You could buy salt, tobacco, small fish, hot peppers and corn (although the black market price for this was alarmingly high). Or you could falsely report that someone had come from home in order to buy guest food rations, and if you couldn't barter for them, or had no money to buy them, you could always steal them. But first you had to forget about 'face'. That had to be cast off to some other realm.

The countenances of people I've written about now float before me. Not one of them is animated – they are as hard and impassive as fish heads. Zhou was a doctor, a graduate of a prestigious college, who was famous in the camp for having found a wild rabbit leg to eat. Later, he was able to put some distance between himself and the Big Troop when he was assigned to work in the State Farm Hospital. At the time of this diary, this good fortune had not yet occurred – he was stationed together with me in the same group. He had a round face and strongly astigmatic eyes. His thick glasses made his look peculiarly large, like a cat. Also like a cat, he was quick and nimble: his expertise in 'eating greens' may even have surpassed his medical abilities.

After being discovered stealing tomatoes, sunflower seeds or sweet potatoes, he would put them aside and do a most sincere self-examination. When that was over, he would immediately go and steal some more. This is what made the Troop Leader call him a bad egg. In terms of human nature, however, he was upright and honest – he even dared to debate with the Troop Leader, dared to refuse to accept his point of view. Troop Leader Zheng probably knew that Zhou was nearing the day when he would be through his sentence and out of the camp, and that he might as well be tolerated.

Heh Deng, my Group Leader at this time, was a highly qualified engineer. At a glance you could see that he didn't have an artistic cell in his body, but his powers of rational thinking were exceptional. If you put proper clothes on him and sent him to an international conference, he would not cause the Chinese people the slightest embarrassment. As recorded in the diary, on 11 September he was making a small iron stove 'with all his soul'. He was dissatisfied with a temporary earthen structure for cooking his greens and sweet potatoes. The iron had come from rusty sheeting over the pigpen; he also stole several rods from the railing that kept in piglets and planned to use them as the grate. In the morning he first told the others what their work was to be for that day, then he argued for a while, and then he put his head down and got busy at banging out his self-appointed task. His focused approach was similar to how he might have done his experiments in the lab.

After a while, he produced a superior portable iron stove. But just as he was preparing to give its belly a final coating of plaster, he was found out by the convict who managed the pigpen.

'Dogshitter! Look at you! I said to myself, "How have all the piglets got out?" and just look, now I see it was this scum who took down the rails! Come on – we're going to your Troop Leader to hear what he has to say.'

The Troop Leader instantly confiscated the results of Heh's scientific experiment. Since Heh Deng was Group Leader, though, the Troop Leader didn't scold him too badly.

Even today the sight of Heh Deng shouting back at that pigpen convict is clearly imprinted on my brain. It was almost as though it had been scripted for a movie. His body took the exact shape of the character *da*, or 'big', except that one foot touched the ground while the other stomped up and down in the air above it. He was incapable of any really good vulgar swearing, so all he could do was shake both arms out to the sides. He looked like an electric pole with jolts of power running down the wires in either direction. A maths book had turned into a kind of cartoon.

Earlier, Heh Deng had mobilized all the convicts in the group to demand that I be disciplined for my ignorance in the thinning of sugar-beet sprouts. Since I became his Secretary General, however, our relationship improved. The diary reflects this. None the less, I have to mention that his most recent actions betrayed something not quite right in his mental state. This became apparent after the amateur philosopher committed suicide: Heh Deng argued with the members of the group, he talked back to the Group Leader, he 'ate greens', he wrote a report resigning his position, he spread negative attitudes. From time to time he even lay down and refused to work, to the point that our entire group was reprimanded for it.

In the labour camps, 'death was a common occurrence'.* Suicide, on the other hand, was extremely rare. So far as I can remember there were only two cases, a tiny percentage of all those who died. It was natural for people who were suffering to think at times that it was better to die than keep on living. I entertained this thought myself. But Chinese intellectuals are a little like Shakespeare's Hamlet. After 'to be or not to be: that is the question' come all kinds of unending doubts. In the camps, the result was that often a man had not quite made up his mind about committing suicide before he went ahead and died of extremity anyway.

Once, when I stayed in the infirmary of the labour reform camp, I slept next to a convict who would sigh long sighs from his deathbed. 'If I had known I'd die this way, I'd have died that way,' he would say. By 'died that way' he meant commit suicide.

'Well then,' I asked him, 'why didn't you die that way?'

'Didn't have time!' he replied.

This phrase struck me as a most enlightening lesson. The inference in it contained the deepest Zen philosophy. This one sentence was probably more profound and accurate than all the other things he had said in his life.

'Didn't have time!' How many 'didn't have times' are there in one person's life! This sentence, like a Rinzai shout and blow, has enabled me to cut through and come

* From a quote by Mao.

to terms with many things. It has made my character considerably more decisive.

Many people 'did not have time' to commit suicide before dying, so successful suicides were hard to accomplish and considered quite rare. Although this suicide ostensibly did not affect the other convicts, the fact that the man had done it, and done it just when he had eaten his fill and practically before the eyes of his wife, could not but have an unconscious effect on us all. Heh Deng's abnormal behaviour resulted, I believe, from the shock of this event.

When on 4 September Troop Leader Zheng went wild with his rope in the field, swinging and hitting everyone he saw, when he ordered our group to stay behind and 'add a night session', Ma Weixiao correctly noted that his punishment of us was a reflection of his own state of mind. 'This devil is taking it hard himself,' he murmured as he continued to scythe through the grass. 'He's got a stomachful of anger and is directing it at us.'

Even the Old Commissar acted out of character by doing everything he could to take care of the dead man's wife and child. He not only refrained from 'capping'* the dead man with the major indictments of 'committing suicide to avoid punishment', 'resisting reform', etc., but he broke convention by asking the carpenter's shed to make the dead man that lovely coffin. This coffin gave his unfortunate yet virtuous wife at least a modicum of spiritual comfort, and at the same time the Old Commissar allowed her to be put up at the infirmary. When she

---

* Labelling a person with the name of an offence, requiring punishment.

had recovered a bit, he paid the expenses for mother and daughter to go home.

I find that as I gaze upon the faces of these cadres, like looking at old photographs through the mists of time, not a single one provokes any feeling of repulsion or hatred. On the contrary, I remember each cadre who was my boss with a certain measure of warmth. The Old Commissar lived on into the 1980s; after he retired he and I lived in the same city. When I was completely rehabilitated and became a so-called author, I would often see him strolling through the streets. His posture was the same as it had been when he was surveying the fields of his domain – body bent over as though he had rickets, hands behind his back, grandly pacing and carefully surveying each green tree and electric pole. Once when he was waiting to cross the street, he happened to have stopped before a huge advertisement that read 'Coca-Cola'. When I saw this, an unutterable feeling of sadness welled up inside me.

The cadres were no better than we were, but neither were they worse. We were not, in fact, any worse than they, but neither were we any better. We were all of us simply men.

By the frequency of references to him in the diary, Troop Leader Zheng appeared to be the most antagonistic towards me of the men in the camps. I seemed to be the mote in his eye, the thorn in his flesh – he appeared to want very much to pluck me out and have done with me. Yet this most severe of Troop Leaders had originally been a convict himself. In 1958 we actually stirred our soup spoons together in the same food bucket in the same group. He, too, was an intellectual and from the same home country as me. Back then, we had a fairly good relationship.

As I remember, he had a pale complexion, eyes with a single fold in the eyelid and thick heavy lips that gave people an impression of sincerity. In 1958, we convicts were still able to get just about enough to eat, and he seemed as happy as if he was still in an office doing administrative work. He put a lot into his duties, and every time there was a 'Thought Line-up' his name came first. He never talked about why he had been sent to the camp – he would just smile if anyone asked. He would often have peanuts in his pockets when we went to the fields in the winter – every time he finished hauling a basket of manure he would throw a peanut in his mouth and laugh aloud as he chewed.

'Delicious! These are the reward they send me from home.'

One day he was promoted from convict to manager of convicts, a Troop Leader. The authorities just shifted his name from one list to the other. He may not have anticipated this himself, and the convicts were even more perplexed. This promotion to the stars in one leap was unrelated to any 'reform' one could point to; it was not something anybody could struggle to achieve through thought reform or even plain hard work.

Soon all was revealed. Zheng had originally been teaching in an agricultural mechanization college. When the school needed to fulfil its responsibilities in the anti-rightist campaign in 1958, they put his name on the list in order to come up with the right number. (No wonder he never talked about his case – there was no case to talk about.) Then the head of the school was also found to be a 'rightist'. According to solid evidence filed against him, he was a real, honest-to-goodness rightist, not just a name to fill in a list. With him, the school's anti-rightist responsibility was now over-fulfilled. The new top man was a soft-headed generous sort of man. Since the quota was already filled, he agonized for a while about sending a blameless man to do hard labour and finally he asked the judicial department to change Zheng's verdict. It was inconvenient to bring Zheng back as a teacher, however, so the school asked him to go home and find some other kind of work.

The labour reform troop was given orders from above to release him. Only then did they learn that this most sterling example of model reform had never done anything bad for which to atone. He had admitted his crime and accepted the punishment, his work performance was impeccable, but in fact he had never committed a crime. Zheng was instantly regarded as a great treasure – the state farm urged him to stay on and be a cadre.

To this day I don't know what he thought about this himself. Perhaps he had a premonition of what was to come. Perhaps he knew that there were raging political movements on the way that would continue to hurt innocent people, that going home to that risk was worse than staying in the relative security of the camp. Perhaps he still felt some kind of primal response to the call of the Party. 'Go where the mother country needs you, go to the hardest place.' In any event, he rejected the chance to return to the phoenix-embroidered beauty of Jiangsu and decided to stay in a primitive, isolated north-west labour camp as a convict boss.

As soon as he became a managerial cadre, this former intellectual convict changed his stripes. He had rolled out of a pile of convicts himself, so there was no hope of trying to deceive him. He knew the wiles and the psychology of intellectuals better than anyone. He had been educated in convict crime school, had been trained and toughened by actual experience, so to convicts he now became a kind of devil.

When I was transformed from the primitive outlying Station Four to headquarters, my heart sank when I learned that Zheng was Troop Leader there. 'Lost,' I cried inside. Earlier I had opened up and told him how I really felt. Now he was Troop Leader, and although he did not expose me, he would often gaze at me with those dark intelligent eyes. His glance was enough to skewer a man and make the skin on his head start to crawl.

On 8 September, my chest hurt and the coughing was worse, so I carried a few less sweet potatoes in my back-basket. With one hand on his hip, the other playing with the rope, making it dance, he yelled at me about how I hadn't rid myself of my superior attitude. At the same time, he told Group Leader Heh Deng to have all the convicts in the group keep a watch on me, on the sly.

When we got home and Heh told me about Zheng confiscating his stove, he added, 'I don't know who put what in his eyes, but when you're around Troop Leader Zheng you'd better be a perfect gentleman.' I knew what he meant. But Zheng didn't need anyone else's eyedrops – his eyes always flashed crystal clear. Naturally I couldn't write this in the diary. A solution, I felt, was to write a poem whole-heartedly praising someone at a higher level than Zheng. I had better open someone else's eyes in order to counter any reports about me that he might be submitting to the authorities.

Other Troop Leaders were the opposite of Troop

Leader Zheng. I can't fail to mention one here whose name does not appear in the diary. He was tall and powerfully built, with a deeply lined square face. His hands were like big fans – a shovel looked like an ivory toothpick in them. His feet were like the hooves of a camel, particularly in their home-made shoes that had been handstitched with heavy cord. When he walked it was as though he was stomping down an earthen foundation – as in the saying, he really could make the mountains shake. When I first saw him that year I wondered if Muslin or Uighur blood ran in his veins. An image of him rises before me every time I write a novel that describes a peasant village.

He was originally just a regular peasant from H County. In the early 1950s, he and his neighbours would help each other plant their fields. He had no idea that this was 'peasants voluntarily organizing themselves in socialist agricultural collectives', nor that Chairman Mao happened to be searching for examples of this practice throughout the country. The leaders of the province discovered him from a newspaper report and immediately conferred on him the title of Model Worker. They sent him to Beijing to attend the Conference of Heroes.

When the Old Commissar started his project of establishing a huge labour reform camp on this patch of swamp in H County, the troops he brought in to work on it were all from elsewhere. He needed a person familiar with local agriculture to serve as a consultant. So they fastened on this man named Ma. From peasant farmer he was swiftly elevated to cadre. He often remarked to the convicts in a most self-satisfied way, 'Better off as a cadre! There's always something to eat!'

Troop Leader Ma was truly an 'official of considerable

merit' in the camp. He became the Commissar's right arm and left arm as well. In those days, if we caught sight of the Old Commissar in the fields, on the roads, on the threshing field, holding meetings, following right behind his rump would be Ma's camel hooves. Sometimes Ma led the men to work, but he never took along a rope to use as a whip. In the field he would get right in there with the convicts, doing whatever work they did. When we were hauling dirt, he would do the harder shovelling part. He would place a shovelful that was seven or eight or ten jin in a convict's basket as lightly as a feather – he'd lift the tremendous weight of earth high and put it down gently. When the person hauling this load found it too heavy to move, Ma would make fun of him.

'Dogshitter! Try this and see how it feels. Is grain good to eat? Work for it!'

If we were digging out a canal or cleaning out silt, everyone prayed he would not be in charge. We were better off with someone who used a rope. The troops used to use a kind of tape measure to mark out how much work we had to do in a day. This invariably broke as it was dragged back and forth, so that soon the extent of a day's piece of work had to rely on the length of stride of the man in charge. Two legs seemed a reliable measure – they didn't break. But an ordinary regular stride of Ma would be twice as long as that of any other Troop Leader. The required work allocation per convict per day was ten strides, so when Ma was in charge the ten became twenty – the work had magically increased one hundred per cent. Digging from morning to night, till you were dizzy from exhaustion, you would still never be able to get it done.

There was one advantage in working for this man. In 1958, at the time of the Great Leap Forward, three meals a day were sent down to the fields for the men to eat. When other Troop Leaders saw that the cart had finished doling out food they would immediately start rounding up people to start work again.

'Into the fields! Into the fields! You're not mincing little gentlemen – you should be able to eat a meal in two or three bites. Move it!'

Convicts served last had to cram food in their mouths as fast as they could. But if Troop Leader Ma happened to be in charge, he would not get everyone moving again until the last convict had finished eating.

'Take it easy when you eat,' he advised. 'Don't gulp! Lightning doesn't strike an eating man!' Or he might say, 'The purpose of life is to be able to eat! Nothing else is as important! Lightning may strike an unfilial son but it waits until he's finished eating his meal!'

He raised eating to sacred heights that could not be violated by a saint or even a ghost.

He also liked to crack jokes when he worked with the convicts and he particularly liked it when convicts who had committed male-female relations* talked about how to handle women. Convicts who had any knowledge at all in this area naturally catered to his tastes. Once he led the convicts out to dig the canal and when he had finished digging his own stretch he squatted by the bank and began chatting with one of the rougher men about various items used in sex. The convict began to teach him about a device made from the sewn-up eyelid of a

---

* Vague in definition, but one of the crimes for which one could be sent into the camps.

sheep – he said that this would invariably make women come to orgasm quickly. I listened from the sidelines, amazed at the creativity of my fellow countrymen. Ma must never have heard of this device either, for he got so excited he jumped right down into the bed of the canal and told the man to keep on talking while he did the man's digging for him. When Ma had heard all there was to hear, and couldn't get too much happier, he rolled over on his back like a child, laughing with his two feet in the air.

As soon as the policy of lowered-rations-to-be-substituted-with-gourds-and-greens started, this peasant became a firm opponent of the Old Commissar. Now, when the Old Commissar made his reports at the head of the group of convicts, Ma would lie down below and make trouble. The Old Commissar would be up there at the front of the threshing group gesticulating as he preached to the convicts, exhorting them to work harder.

'Work as hard as you used to suck on your mother's tit!' he would yell.

Ma would be squatting among the convicts like a big brown bear, grumbling to the men around him, 'Balls! Keeps telling people to work harder! If you don't give a man enough to eat, where's he going to get the strength? Tits?! Nobody's tits have anything to suck! Where's the milk? No milk! Let him suck his mother's shrivelled tit himself!'

I should clarify that it is impossible to put in written language the dialect that came from Ma's mouth. Every sound he produced had a peculiar ring to it, as if the sound wasn't produced in his throat but was formed by the twisting and shaping of his lips and jaw. They managed to give his words a startling vigour. He never used declarative sentences. His grumbling didn't cover up the hoarse shout of the Old Commissar, but it was loud enough to be heard by nearby convicts and often by the Old Commissar himself. According to the rules, the Troop Leader in charge of a given Group was supposed to accompany them to keep order when they were assembled to hear reports. The Old Commissar soon learned to assign Ma to work somewhere else, rather than let him sing a contrary tune below.

After we started the regimen of lowered rations, Ma became like a benign sheep-herder when he led us out to work. In the early morning he'd take us to the appointed workplace, but whether we worked or not was all the same to him. His strides were just as long when we dug the canal, but now it didn't matter if we never finished. When the sun went down behind the mountains he would yell out that it was time to quit.

He'd say to the convicts that he respected (for example, those rascals who knew how to handle women), 'Back in the old society when a landlord wanted to hire temporary hands, a band of poor folk would suddenly materialize around him! Landlord wouldn't know who could work, who couldn't! Who was strong, who wasn't! How'd he figure it out? He'd tell someone to bring a big basket of steamed buns for them to eat! Whoever ate the most got hired! Why? Those with bigger stomachs for eating have more energy! But now? Balls!' He would twist his head and curl his lip in an expression of contempt.

Sometimes he would walk up to convicts who were working and say, as if to ridicule them, 'Had enough to eat? Dogshitter, give me a straight answer!' Who dared say in public, especially in front of a Troop Leader, that

41

he was hungry? The criminal convicts could bare their yellow teeth at him in a cheeky laugh. Intellectual convicts could neither say they were hungry nor that they were full, so they might mumble something about how they were getting along.

Then his anger would erupt. 'Getting along! You people who can read are really motherfucking word-spinners! Full is full! Empty is hungry! What's this "getting along"? You dogshitters deserve to be hungry!'

I once ran away, in 1959, when summer was just turning into fall, and within the space of one day ate three hemp bags full of watermelon, and my exploit became an after-dinner anecdote among the cadres. When Ma heard it he came out to the field specifically to see me – he wanted to look at this watermelon-eating pro. When he saw my emaciated state he actually praised me to the Troop Leader on duty. 'This dogshitter shows promise – he's going to be something some day. Never mind what a wreck he looks now! Three hemp bags of watermelon in a day! Ha ha!' Slapping his thighs, he rocked back and forth with laughter.

If he was this reckless in letting loose with counter-revolutionary talk before the convicts, you can imagine what he was like among the cadres. Yet there wasn't a cadre who dared to contradict or criticize or expose him. His 'roots were proper, his sprouts were red'. His ancestors had been poor peasants for eight generations and more. Besides, who else had ever seen Chairman Mao? The Old Commissar was already part of the Revolution in the early 1930s, but he had enjoyed no more than a distant sighting of Chairman Mao at Yan'an. This Troop Leader Ma, on the other hand, had not only seen Chairman Mao at the Conference of Heroes, he had even shaken Chairman Mao's hand. He had had a picture taken with him!

During cadre meetings he alone dared to say counter-revolutionary things openly before the Old Commissar, and the Old Commissar could do no more than scold him with a smile. 'Old Ma, your damn mouth never takes a break and it says some very peculiar things!' Ma was allowed to roam at will outside the rules.

One day, however, we convicts were out cleaning the silt from a canal. We were lined up in a straight line down its middle. I had my head down, doing the stretch I'd been assigned to. Today wasn't Ma's day to oversee us but all of a sudden he was there on the bank. His darkly tanned face was black with anger and he was spitting like an erupting volcano. He pointed at us and abused us, working from one end of the canal to the other.

'Which of you dogshitters blinded the dog's eye? Wants to knock over his grandfather! Forget it! What does your grandfather do to eat? There's not a good one among you motherfucking scribes. You're all bastards! No conscience! I'll never let any son of mine learn to read! Soon as you know writing you lose your own basic nature. Motherfuckers would report their grandfather! Right to the labour reform bureau! Think your grandfather's afraid of that? Said No! Not afraid! What's this "counter-revolutionary talk"? Dogshitters go off and report all you want! Best of all report right up to Chairman Mao! You think your grandfather'd be afraid of that? Screw all you book-readers! The words you've read just get stuffed into dog's stomachs. The ink has blackened your hearts! I curse all you book-readers!'

His eyes were bloodshot as he paced back and forth

43

on the bank. He would race over to an intellectual convict and point at him while he cursed. When he saw me his finger moved abruptly away from the top of my head, as though someone who could eat several hemp bags full of watermelon in one day could not be considered a real book-reader. From his mouth came the most abstruse, marvellous and audacious things. Without the slightest immodesty he described the various ways he had used their mothers to bring these very book-readers into existence. I learned a number of superb folk sayings from him at this time. They summed up mankind's experience of sex all the way from the beginning down to modern man. This was truly a treasury of knowledge accumulated over tens, even hundreds of thousands of years. From a sociological standpoint we were hearing the vestiges of an ancient fertility worship. Historians or ethnologists could have written numerous scholarly dissertations based on this. It's a shame I can't quote all these things in my writing.

The Troop Leader in charge stood to one side on the canal bank with his arms folded, laughing as hard as he could and not making a move to stop him. Ma cursed and ranted till he was completely worn out. Then, like a bull camel that has just mounted a female, with extended nostrils, puffing crude snorts, he turned around and strode back to Headquarters.

We convicts stood in the middle of the canal, holding our shovels, looking at each other and wondering what to make of this explosion.

From then on, he never led the men to work again. He was transferred to a manager's job in the cadre's mess hall. Apparently the Old Commissar had decided to separate him from the convicts. It was sufficient punishment to make a man who couldn't even read the numbers 1, 2, 3, 4 work with account books. Shortly afterwards, the Old Commissar assigned a middle school student to assist him and then he had even less to do. When we went out to work we would see him squatting by the road, watching us with doleful, even envious eyes as we headed for his beloved open fields.

Free convicts were always the main source of information in the big yard of the camp, and you could be confident that the news they passed along was absolutely accurate, more so than that of any reporter today. They didn't dare say anything that lacked a firm basis in reality. If something was later traced back and found to have been fabricated, the free convict would be accused of starting counter-revolutionary rumours and would be punished accordingly.

At one point the free convicts passed along the information that our old peasant Troop Leader Ma, who worshipped eating and was against making us work on too little food, had been turned in not by the Old Commissar or one of his own comrades. Instead, he had been done in by one of his hungry convicts. The document accusing him had been cleverly handled. Instead of being passed directly to the Old Commissar – for everyone knew of their good relationship – it had been given to a relative to take out of the camp. That way it could safely be mailed to authorities of the labour reform bureau at the provincial level. This guaranteed that higher authorities would pass it back down to our camp with an order to take action.

The unimaginable part of this was that the informer was not seeking merit points for himself, or even to make a name for himself. It was an anonymous letter, merely signed 'one who has committed Thought Mistakes'. The letter said that this Thought Offender truly and honestly wanted to purge the ranks of cadres of hidden bad people. He could no longer allow the convicts in their labour reform to be subjected to a certain bad influence. Whoever opposed Chairman Mao's enlightened policy of lowered-rations-to-be-substituted-with-gourds-and-greens should be punished.

From then on, every time I have met a person who humbly says that he has committed Thought Mistakes, my conditioned reflex has been to excuse myself and politely move away. I have learned the hard way. An intellectual may have good motives and start with a clear sense of reality. But after undergoing repeated struggle-and-criticism sessions in a highly politicized environment he will be unable to keep from feeling that his thinking must indeed have problems. Eventually he will decide that he must wake up and face his mistakes. Then, through bitter hardship, after reforming what was not wrong in the first place, he will lose track of himself and lose a grounding in reality. In Troop Leader Ma's words, he will do harm to his own basic nature. Traumatized by ever more frightening darkness, in the end he will reach a point where he has lost his humanity. It is more dangerous to be around this kind of intellectual than it is to walk among wolves after nightfall in the deepest mountains.

12 *September*

Still in the north pigpen. Heh Deng complained and spread unrest among the new arrivals (about grain not being enough, about Group Leader Chen, etc.). After work, pulling the cart along the road, Bai, Lu, and Du reported to Chen on the matter. Chen told us to write up some documentation on it. When?! That evening Bai wrote a piece and asked me to sign. I couldn't help but sign.

13 *September*

Hauled dirt in the morning in north pigpen. At rest time, Station Leader Yan and Division Director Gao came to the work site to lecture us. Mainly it was to denounce old convicts for poisoning the minds of new convicts. Also, three people were struggled against (Ren, Peng, Guang). They had each hauled only sixty jin of earth per cart. At eleven o'clock they suddenly left to have their lunch. Bai and I surmised there would be another large meeting in which people would be arrested. After eating we were told to gather at the big meeting ground, but not until four o'clock did they formally and officially convene the meeting. It was indeed a large meeting for giving out punishment. They arrested fifty or sixty people. Lu Xizhi, Tao Qiu, Xu Hanzhang were all arrested for the crime of refusing to reform. This was the accomplishment of the Double Counter Movement. State Farm Leader Wen also reported that a certain group of men would graduate in a few days.

Studied in the evening; a joint meeting of groups struggled against Guang Tingbi, then dragged out Lin Bingkun, saying he had talked back to Troop Leader Zheng. Lin tried to explain over and over but it was no use.

14 *September*

Hauled dirt in north pigpen. Deng Wende said something that scared me. When his Group Leader was sick, the Troop Leader asked him to take charge. He allowed people to do what they wanted and so they developed a negative attitude toward work. I don't think he has any fundamental counts against himself personally so in fact should be all right.

Troop Leader Zheng gave Heh a lecture. Heh didn't work all morning. I hauled the cart; so tired my chest hurt even more. Afternoon I asked to be allowed to work in the pigpen.

Evening was study session to reorganize our group. It was led by Group Leaders Chen and Lin. Liu Xueru, Zhu Zhenbang, Liu Fengxiang, Feng Guozuo spoke. All brought up the problem of Heh Deng. All talked about his dissatisfaction with the current situation, eating greens, causing negative work habits, etc. A lot of it was fact, some was related to fact. Not sure why, but Troop Leader Zheng specifically appointed me as secretary to take notes for this meeting.

15 September

The meeting yesterday went on until ten p.m. They said we could rest this morning, but after breakfast came the call to go to work. The new arrivals really do work well – we old convicts are left in their dust. May be two reasons: they just got in, so bodies are more resilient; and their socialist education has been more thorough than ours. A lot of their drive comes from political training.

Evening was another study meeting. Sick, couldn't attend. The case against Heh Deng moved to the next step. Troop Leader Zheng said this was just a start – later there would be others. I was close to Heh, so should now draw a clear line between us, not get myself tainted. Prepared to make a statement the next day. Troop Leader Zheng appointed Su Qin as Group Leader; Heh Deng was retired from his post to do some self-reflecting.

The sheds we had been constructing one after another since July were now receiving their long-awaited guests.

Starting in early September, each day brought in wave after wave of new convicts and great activity to the big yard of the camp. In the eyes of these new arrivals I was an old convict myself now, and we old convicts were all quite glad to see these new recruits. The happiest were those greeting colleagues or bosses who had rectified them in the past. These men had now been marked as 'bad people' themselves and sentenced to hard labour in the camps.

'Welcome! Welcome! Department Chief X X-x, we welcome your auspicious arrival to this place!'

One day, coming back from work, we poured through the big yard and one of us saw his Department Chief squatting at the foot of the wall holding his head in misery. Taking off his hat, the old convict paid this new arrival his respects. The Department Chief wept and refused to raise his head. When it was time to eat, to celebrate the occasion the old convict generously divided up his grass soup and distributed it to the others.

'Damn! We have good leaders after all! They took revenge for me! Revenge! Revenge! None of you knew this man's arrogance back then. Dogshitter, he too was bound to have his day. Who wants food! Who wants some food! Today old Lao-zi gives his food to whomever he meets!'

The leaders he applauded weren't the heads of his work unit but rather the highest powers in the country, those who had started the Double Counter Movement.

They can truly be said to have made manifest the Way of Heaven. Those rectifying others were in the end rectified themselves; those hurting others were hurt themselves. The net of Heaven may have large holes in it but it lets nothing through. Retribution was made possible by the continuous political movements put into motion by our highest leaders, until in the end everyone had his turn.

As the saying goes, 'When enemies meet, their eyes get red.' Troop Leader Zheng did not allow old convicts to beat up new convicts, but just to see opponents fall into the same misfortune made earlier arrivals glad. During this period convicts who were given such opportunity to be glad were in a distinct majority.

The next most fortunate ones were old convicts who finally had the chance to meet up again with relatives and old friends. It was extraordinary to come back from work and discover your colleague or friend, or father, son, brother, wife or husband sitting there below the wall that surrounded us. He or she was not there for a visit, but rather to be one among you, to be 'reformed all together'. Only those who have personally experienced this emotion can know what it felt like. It is perhaps best described as grief intermingled with joy.

On seeing an old hand at labour reform, the newly arrived friend or relative would take every opportunity, during eating or lining up or in the short time between Small Group meetings, to find a quiet place and hurriedly exchange a few words. Where in the camp could be considered quiet? The exact same foot of the same surrounding wall. People crouched there two by two, talking softly and urgently. One had to relay quickly all the hard-earned lessons in how to survive here, also to learn how relatives were doing on the outside, also to say, 'You've just come in . . . did you bring anything to eat? You're not really hungry yet . . . give me a little!'

Fall has always been a customary time for families to get together for a reunion in China. It is a beautiful season, and just at this time a number of family members were indeed reunited by the Double Counter Movement. I can still name by name no less than twenty pairs of fathers and sons or wives and husbands who were sent, first one then the other, to the camps. They include Lei Yuan'en, now professor in Yinchuan's Party School, also Ma Fengying, Xian Kangli, Ms Zhang Ruobing who was formerly professor in Yinchuan's Middle School Nine, Professor Yao Lizhang, now passed away, and others. These people generously provided me with their own valuable recollections, and I would like to extend my profound appreciation to them here.

The reunion that moved me most, and that I remember to this day, was that of a father and son whose names I don't even know.

The son was a thoroughly nondescript young man of around twenty. The minute you saw his gait you knew that he was accustomed to herding sheep in the mountains. This kind of person was not sent in to do labour reform on account of ideological mistakes or problems in political thinking. He was either a petty thief or the sort of criminal that had no clear-cut crime – even the court that sentenced him could not give a precise reason. His face exhibited the effects of in-breeding. From broad cheekbones a small chin receded into his neck, very like a plaster of Paris model of Peking Man.*

* Peking Man is said to date from around five hundred thousand years ago.

It was the sort of face that gave people an impression of stupid honesty.

Like a sheep in a flock he was never the first nor the last – he had never been praised, nor had he been criticized. We were not in the same group and I was unlikely ever to do any trading with him – if it had not been for the fact that his father was also sent into the camps, I would probably never have noticed him.

On that day in September, though, when we were coming back from work, piling through the gate, everyone glanced around the big yard as usual to see if any new arrivals had come in. I saw this young man suddenly head towards an old Han* squatting there. I heard him softly say the word 'Father'. The two of them then sat tightly pressed against each other. They didn't talk; they spoke through their eyes as father gazed at son. Such a familial warmth flowed from the scene that the big yard no longer seemed to be set in a labour reform camp. Apart from their surroundings, they could have been mistaken for a father visiting his son in school.

After harvest, during the idle season, convicts had nearly one hour of their own time in between queuing up for the evening soup and the start of Small Group meetings. I always used that time to run over to the infirmary to try to negotiate half-rest or full-rest status. Even if unsuccessful, I could generally manage to get a few sweet-grass pills or some ferrous sulphate. When I was there, I saw the two of them daily in the same place at the foot of the wall. They ate together there – the son would spoon out a fresh green leaf from his soup bowl

---

* Old man, but specifically Chinese as opposed to Muslim, who are common in the north-west.

into his father's. The father would dredge out a lump of undissolved flour and give it to his son. After eating each would lick his bowl clean and the father would then roll a cabbage leaf into a cigarette. He would smoke this with obvious relish while his son, like a good child, amused himself with a branch, wobbling back and forth on his heels herding imaginary sheep.

At times father and son would plait the liners for back-baskets together. With a liner the basket wouldn't rub the spine as badly when hauling dirt or manure. The father's experienced hands, rough as bark themselves, would rub the *ji-ji* grass and bark. The son would hand the father scraps of fabric, bit by bit, as though acting out his role in a play. None of these bits of fabric was larger than the size of a palm – even so, valuable scraps like this could only be found in the trash behind the dormitories of cadres' families. The large pile of scraps that father and son worked from must have been gathered at great danger as they ventured into forbidden cadre territory. When the back-basket itself was constructed and the patchy multicoloured lining was sewn securely in place, the father would fit it snugly to his son's shoulders as though fitting a new suit of clothes. The son would bend at the waist and, like an ancient primate, turn a few circles to see where there might still be spine-rubbing places.

Even an old convict like me had never seen anyone use his rest time to organize the tools of his labour-reform trade. The two of them were conscientious and focused, as if this were their real home and they were working their own fields.

The day finally arrived that people had so looked forward to – Mid-Autumn Festival, symbolizing the day families joined together in celebration. All of autumn seemed to glow in anticipation of this one day. Convicts were not assembled to listen to reports that evening, since the Troop Leaders had all gone home for a holiday. We were allowed to roam the big yard at will. The moon that night was so round it was like a great white bun and the very smell of cooking seemed to come from its rays of light. As I strolled beneath it, I imagined that it had been sent to hang above me by my mother. I thought of it as a brilliantly shiny package from the postman.

Suddenly I saw the two of them, father and son, shoulder to shoulder, motionless at the foot of the wall. Their heads were lifted, gazing at that mesmerizing moon. The young Peking Man and the ancient enchanting moon exchanged the unspoken light of recognition. He could have been perched on a platform before a mountain cave. His howl from hundreds of thousands of years ago had passed through history to arrive at this place, this time, to become a lingering, unending note in an ongoing song. The father, silent, emaciated, his face crossed with wrinkles, seemed in a state of intoxicated satisfaction with the world. He was full of a kind of gratitude toward fate, also full of gratitude towards the people who had directed his fate.

These two were fundamentally unthinking. They did not try to figure out who was right and who was wrong, they did not put up any resistance, nor were they remotely concerned about the 'direction of Society'. They were like running water flowing with the current of their lives, so that what happened to be convenient turned into fate itself. For better or worse, they had already achieved the state of mind that the sixth Zen patriarch, Hui Neng, propounded more than one thousand years ago. 'Think no good, think no evil' was to them a superfluous lesson, and as a result they exhibited the primordial nature of man. Their two pale, malnourished faces reflected the greenish-white of the moon. They seemed almost to have entered into the moonlight, so that I could not but envy them and be moved.

To this day my heart starts to pound when I think of that state of mind. A part of me wants to achieve that primitive condition, to cast off the self-absorption of today. Only then can one float with the tide, be at ease with whatever comes and know true repose. That state of mind probably epitomizes the round completeness, the perfection, of Buddhism. On the other hand, even back then I had the glimmering of a new understanding. We had been told by the highest leader in the land to learn from the poor peasant class. What he appeared to mean was this attitude of acceptance. That is, this willingness to abide by whatever they, the leaders, put forth; this willingness to be manipulated by others. I was beginning to comprehend that, even as I watched this father and son.

Why was I so glad that more people were being sent in to join us? I met neither old opponents nor enemies in the big yard (I have never considered anyone my enemy although it seems there were people willing to regard me as theirs). Nor did I ever meet up with old friends or relatives. No, I welcomed others to help carry the burden.

If all the pressures of society were borne by just a few of us, then we would have been crushed long ago. With more of us it was safer; as the saying goes, 'If heaven falls, the one who is tallest will hold it up.' By now, the weight I could manage to bear had been sorely diminished, almost to zero. After the deployment of the Double Counter Movement, more and more people were sent in to be labour reform convicts and I consequently felt my burden growing lighter.

A supreme attribute of our society at that time was its ability to make every individual shoulder a portion of political pressure. This turned out to be even more fairly distributed than the apportionment of material goods. This excellent trait came to its ultimate expression during the Great Cultural Revolution when the Great Leader's talent in dividing up political pressure was even more precise than my ability to portion out food, to the point that it reached absolute equality.

Secondly, there was a tendency for both old convicts and Troop Leaders to rise in status in comparison with the new arrivals. The feeling was that the first bad people were hauled into the camps because their badness was obvious. Since it was obvious it was, para-doxically, superficial. Those people who had to be dug out and exposed later had clearly been lurking in deeper places – why else would they make the people, the masses, go to such lengths to dig them out?! These later arrivals were clearly more 'bad', in fact they were the real 'bad elements'. Their badness also had a different complexion to it. As a result, old labour reform convicts shared a sense of superiority to new arrivals. At the very least we had not made people go to great lengths to ferret us out.

And so I welcomed the new convicts with enthusiasm. Group Leader Heh was the opposite. He put on a long face whenever he returned from work to find new convicts assigned to our group.

'You're not allowed to ladle water yourselves!' he barked. 'Water's scarce, not enough to drink. Has to be rationed!'

My diary records that the two new convicts who now entered our group were technicians from the Geomorphology Bureau of Yinchuan. From the looks of their lily-white hands and the way they carried a carrying pole, they were desk workers. After Heh's injunction, they waited helplessly beside the water bucket with dry mouths and parched tongues, licking their lips as they looked around for someone to come and ration them some water. This stupid-duck demeanour was extremely funny to us old convicts. Seeing how they were so clearly out of their depth made us realize just what superior old hands we ourselves had become.

The first cause of Heh Deng's unhappiness was that he yet again had to go to the trouble of assigning bunks to new arrivals. Not only was this a lot of work, it also meant that the fifty centimetres we currently enjoyed would be further reduced. A second reason was something he told me just before going to sleep one night. When others were busy with their own affairs he revealed his grievances to his secretary, that is, to me.

'They've sent in all kinds of crap. It really isn't right!'

Under normal conditions a troop would not put convicts from the same unit or from the same case together in one Small Group. This was to prevent their joining forces to form a gang. So how was it that these two cadres from the same bureau came to be stuffed together in our Small Group?

The older of the two was around fifty, very well

groomed and sophisticated but indicted with a serious crime. In 1949 his wife bore him his first son. The virtuous People's Republic of China had just been established and so he gave his son the name 'Love the Country': Ai Guo [Kuo]. The second child was born in September 1954, on the happy occasion of the opening ceremony of the first National People's Congress, and so he gave his second son the name 'Love the People': Ai Min. The third child happened to be born in September 1956, just at the time of the eighth meeting of the Communist Party plenary session, and so he gave this little son the name 'Love the Party': Ai Dang. Now, in 1960, at the start of the Double Counter Movement, the eldest was eleven, the second son was seven, and the youngest was four.

In the labour reform camp each of us was required to write reports exposing two people; out in society the number was undoubtedly much higher. Behind each person's back fluttered many of these exposés. This elegant intellectual, who had this peculiar way of commemorating national events, was now said in one of these exposés to have used the pretext of his children's names to commemorate his own anti-revolutionary sentiments. If you put the three names of the children together they became Love the KuoMinDang (KMT).*

This was a hideously poisonous and very well-concealed plot. People who had worked with this man for years had never even suspected it. Even the officer in charge of registering the whereabouts of everyone knew nothing about it, and he knew almost everything. The

* Kuomindang, the government of the Nationalist Party, which retreated to Taiwan in 1949.

person who wrote the exposé, broke the code, so to speak, and detected the plot was someone who should have received a medal for his acumen.

But 'the mantis stalks the cicada, unaware of the oriole behind it'. Behind the back of the man exposing this gentleman was an exposé on him in return. Among the condemnations of him was written, 'This is a matter so serious, and the counter-revolutionary who names his sons in this way was so very well hidden, that he had to be someone who had a bone-deep hatred of the Party. Anyone who could see through this kind of thinking and break this code had to have the same counter-revolutionary mental makeup.'

The people in the Geomorphology Bureau thought, 'Hey, that's right! We've been involved in the Revolution for a long time, so our revolutionary awareness is pretty high. Plus we can claim considerable discernment and political alertness – why were we not conscious of this? When his children had birthdays we even went to his home to celebrate! We never figured out this thing about the names. It must be that the clever code-breaker had the same evil thoughts: he must be sent to do labour reform as well!'

And so it turned out that two people with the same case type from the same institution were enemies. Putting them together was a way of ensuring mutual surveillance and mutual exposing.

Heh Deng heard the case details of these two men and one might have assumed that, rationalist engineer that he was, he would find them comic and absurd. Instead, he did not feel at all that this pair of opponents had been wronged but that he himself was being ridiculed. 'It's just not right!' This did not mean that society

60

was haphazardly doing wrong to good people but rather that society had taken these 'haphazard people' and stuffed them into his ranks, lowering what he considered to be the high standing of a political prisoner.

Yes, ever since August and the start of the Double Counter Movement, if one were interested enough to ask about the crimes of those who had been 'countered' and poured into the camps, one would find that the cases were generally as follows: somebody stole a half-jin grain coupon from the mess hall, somebody was late in getting to work and always left early, somebody had done nothing more than argue with his old lady, probably upsetting her to the point that she exposed him with some unmentionable crime. Others, when asked, looked at you with hurt and vacuous eyes as if expecting you to tell them what they had done.

In short, if the leaders of a unit Outside did not like the looks of you, or wanted to fire or generally get rid of you, you became a target of the Double Counter Movement. Under the Thought Instruction to 'correctly manage internal contradictions among the people', it was improper to let this kind of person roam freely in society. One could pride oneself on finding an appropriate place in which they could settle down. Official sentencing was just too much trouble. What's more, these 'stir-fried squid' were, after all, not real enemies of the people but merely examples of internal contradictions among the people. They should be allowed to benefit from the nurturing of labour reform. They were duly advised that when they had properly reformed they could graduate, and this conveniently adjustable period was quite beneficial in motivating them to reform.

We old convicts had lost all regard for what we once

61

thought of as the value of a man. We maintained great respect, however, for the virtues of a convict. A convict's respectability was based primarily on what his original crime had been. Depending on how serious it was, he received a different degree of worthiness or standing among the convicts. My crime, for example, had been to publish counter-revolutionary poems. Heh Deng had used the pretext of the Party's rectification movement to attack some Party leaders, plus in the past he had been a member of the 'Three Sweeps Clean Movement'. Ma Weixiao was the filial son and virtuous grandson of the head of a band of Counter Revolutionaries. Zhu Zhenbang was a runaway convict, etc. Every old convict had plenty of qualifications for that difficult-to-attain status of political prisoner.

Those who had committed undefined crimes, like Su Xiaosu or the young Peking Man, were swept into the general category of petty thief. Like students at school who were mere auditors, these people weren't really recognized by your standard convict. Convicts with serious crimes like mine, Heh Deng's, Ma Weixiao's, or that of the historian who liked the taste of toads, were generally accorded the respect of other convicts even if we were not able to become high-class convicts. When convicts talked among themselves about whose crimes were greatest, you could see the admiration in the sideways glance of their eyes. Old convicts may have had stomachs shrivelled with hunger, but we felt good about ourselves and could keep our backs straight.

In order to gain a modicum of standing among other convicts and also to build a sense of self-value, some convicts with no real crime intentionally fabricated the most creative reasons for being sent to the camp. They might even brag about having killed people, set fires etc., so that the public security bureau officials who had sent them in began to regret it: if this had been known earlier, they could have had these people executed!

I began to suspect that most of the new convicts among the waves of men being sent in by the Double Counter Movement were crimeless. As a result, that former sense of superiority by which we judged these men to be 'worse' than we were turned into a loss of our own self-esteem. Having the government send these people into our ranks was the equivalent of ridiculing those of us who had committed real crimes.

Heh Deng was highly educated and had a very clear mind, so as he explained his point of view to me I, too, began to see it that way. As he said, when a brilliant student who has been admitted on the basis of merit sees ignorant scum get into his university he feels angry. What had the camps turned into? Were they nothing more than kindergartens? It just wasn't right!

After the two enemies were assigned to our Small Group on 11 September, we all started waiting for them to continue reporting on each other and stirring up trouble. Maybe they would even get in a fight with each other! Heh Deng turned his nose up at them; Ma Weixiao watched with cold eyes from the sidelines. I, too, carefully monitored their movements at all times. This was not for amusement – how could emaciated men find any energy to entertain themselves? No, it was because as soon as they broke out in a fight we would have real substance for our examination-of-lifestyle meetings. We would not have to make such an effort to find bad traits among ourselves, that is, to find reasons to criticize people with whom we were all quite familiar. Struggling against strangers gave one fewer qualms than struggling against people you knew. Those who were often singled out as targets, Zhu Zhenbang, Fang Aihua, Su Xiaosu and others, hoped even more fervently that the new pair would take their place.

Several days passed, however, and not only had the couple not argued or fought, but they seemed to look after each other. They quickly accommodated themselves to the surroundings, observing with minute and careful caution the various rules of the camp.

When our Small Group worked in the pigpen the two of them hauled the cart, all the while belittling our pen, saying it was not half so well kept and clean as theirs at the Geomorphology Institute. The pigs at their institute were also much healthier than ours, indeed their pigs were more lovable than ours. If there was any hatred between these two it wasn't visible to us – they seemed to have become partners in jointly ridiculing our pigs. The camp's pigpen was indeed a mess, as I wrote in the diary on 9 September: 'Pigs are pitifully thin, but the pen is sturdy.' In the eyes of the new arrivals we old convicts should apparently feel ashamed of ourselves, should perhaps look for a hole to crawl into.

I learned a lot from them, however. I learned that on the Outside every organization now had a plot of land near town on which the staff raised their own food to supplement the lowered rations and shortage of grain. A self-sufficient economic model was beginning to cover the entire country. The Great Leader called upon everyone to 'get involved, mobilize yourselves, do it all yourselves: mend clothes, raise food'. No matter what sort of work a cadre did, he was expected to help in the farmwork and to participate in physical labour to reform his world-view.

This was something that had not existed before I entered the labour reform camp. It seemed that if you were to compare convicts doing labour reform with citizens out in society, the only distinction was that one group could go home at night and the other could not go home. This gave me a small measure of comfort. I now felt that being put into the camp was like being poured from a large bucket into a smaller bucket, not much more. In terms of the broad strokes of fate, there had not been a substantial change.

The two new men had already participated somewhat in the work of the farm managed by the Geomorphology Institute. After two or three days of digging and hauling dirt, they were fairly indistinguishable from the rest of us. This made me even more acutely aware that my seven hundred-odd days of hard labour had been wasted effort. I was inferior to these two men in every way. My physical stamina was not up to theirs, my thinking was certainly not as advanced as theirs, and so I wrote in the diary for 15 September: 'The new arrivals really do work well – we old convicts are left in their dust.' I felt that the reason could only be that they had 'received more socialist education' than we had.

Two events proved that their socialist education was indeed greater. The young geomorphology technician who was so good at breaking codes was named Long Zhenxing. He was short but shrewd. Behind his uplifted eyebrows were a pair of clear eyes that seemed to flash the message that they penetrated the very layers of the earth. On 15 September, Heh Deng assigned the two of us to haul a cart of earth to the pigpen. When we got to the side of the cart he charged ahead to lift the shafts.

'Accountant, you're too weak,' he said. 'Better let me pull the cart.'

This sort of voluntary willingness to do the harder work had long since disappeared from the camp. The title 'accountant' alarmed me as well, with its sense of currying favour. It was the first time I had ever been addressed so respectfully ... at the same time it made me feel somewhat superior. So I impolitely let him pull the shafts. I tied the rope that was attached to the axle around my shoulders and then, shoulder to shoulder, we moved forward. Heh Deng had intended to look after me by assigning us to work together, thinking that I could save a little energy. Who would have known that when the cart was loaded this bastard would take up the shaft, tuck down his head, bend his two strong shoulders against the weight and fly forward! There was no way that I, who could scarcely step over a stalk of rice, could keep up. Instead of helping him pull I was being dragged along by the rope. After two running trips I fell to the ground, panting for breath.

At rest time, he said sympathetically, 'Accountant, how is it you're in such terrible condition? You don't seem to have any strength at all! We may have made mistakes in our thinking, but we still need to keep up physical strength in order to reform! How do you think you can reform if you're like that?!'

Fortunately he regarded himself as having 'made mistakes in his thinking'. Otherwise I might have said frankly that I had no strength because I didn't get enough to eat, that it was an odd malady called starvation. But I recalled what had happened to Troop

66

Leader Ma and restrained myself. Coughing a few times, I finally said, 'I was unhealthy before I came in to do labour reform. In childhood I never got enough of my mother's milk so I'm congenitally deficient.'

He commiserated, clucking sympathetically, then after a moment of silence asked me in a low voice, 'Accountant, if I hear any talk of dissatisfaction to whom should I report it? Which Troop Leader? The one who leads us to work or is there a Troop Leader specifically in charge of Thought Work?'

This zealot was incessantly thinking of telling on people! I had always thought I should learn how to do this, but never succeeded. He probably thought that I also loved turning people in, that I had been elevated to Secretary because of it. He didn't know that my appointment was only because I'd written 'Shine On, Crimson Rays', 'Airplane Sprays Insecticide', and other sycophantic poems. With my chest hurting, I said, 'You've only been here a few days. What sort of complaints have you heard? By whom?'

As he had criticized our pigpen he now began criticizing our 'university'. 'Everyone!' he said. 'It seems to me the Thought Work here isn't anything like as tightly managed as it is on the Outside. Even Small Group Leader Heh complains about things: how there isn't enough water to drink, how there isn't enough grain to eat. He even said that Troop Leader Zheng was a donkey's ass, that all he could do was lash convicts with his rope. Anyway, he said a lot! That's not good. How can he lead us in our Thought Reform if he talks like that?'

I was so disturbed by this that my heart raced and I began to cough uncontrollably. Heh Deng had been the one to mobilize everyone against me when I mistakenly weeded out the best sugar-beet sprouts, but once I had been made Secretary his attitude toward me changed. One benefit of being Secretary was that while others worked I could pretend to be wielding a pencil and doing my secretary job. When it was time for everyone to quit work I would go around with my measuring stick to measure how much grass the convicts had cut or how much dirt they had hauled.

A pile of grass or heap of dirt was measured in terms of volume, which was the *liang-fang* measurement noted in the diary. The measuring stick was actually nothing more than a small branch. As I've said before, the camps, like the entire country, were so poor that even a primitive measuring device was not available. When it was necessary to measure something the Troop Leader had the convicts cut off some relatively straight tree branches to serve as the standard 'metre'. These were then cut to the same length and known as measuring sticks. They were distributed to the accountants of each Small Group.

'Use this to measure, and remember you're forbidden to mess around!'

If the Troop Leader had not made that last comment it would have been fine, but the minute he said it was forbidden to get up to any tricks I was inspired. I secretly cut off a branch of white poplar that was identical in thickness and colour of bark to the special branches we had been issued . . . but I made it shorter by ten centimetres. When measuring I used my own stick; when I saw the Troop Leader approach I would exchange mine for the longer stick he had issued. The efficiency of our Small Group instantly went up by ten per cent.

This trick could fool the Troop Leader but naturally it

didn't get by the Small Group Leader. After Heh Deng discovered it, however, he looked sideways at me and laughed out loud. 'No wonder you're a poet, you bum.' He clapped me on the shoulder. 'You've got some imagination!' His normally serious expression cracked open in the grin of a naughty child. He promptly stopped mobilizing people to have me punished.

We kept this secret between us, which also brought us closer together. Then, on 7 September, after measuring for the Small Group, on the way home I met a neighbouring villager who had been out fishing and I spent two *jiao* to buy his twelve small fish. In order to cook them I needed to go out to get branches for a fire; also I had to search for clods to build a small stove. But as soon as I got home I collapsed in a heap on the bunk – I couldn't make myself do anything more than lie there. Heh Deng instantly noticed the fish I had procured.

Excited, he began to comfort me, saying, 'Let me help! You stay here and rest a while.'

He sped out the door with the fish. In no time at all he had them cooked and brought them back steaming to our Number. I specifically noted in the diary that these were 'small' fish. In fact the largest was no longer than a finger. Naturally you couldn't gut or scale these before cooking or you wouldn't have any fish left. After cooking, the scales, meat and innards alike turned into a dark-grey paste. In order to divide this paste fairly Heh Deng used a small ladle. With rear-end in the air, he bent down by the soot-blackened pan and began to work as exquisitely and carefully as if he had been designing the most complex scientific instrument. First he divided the paste into two roughly equal parts. Then, eyedrop by eyedrop, he evened out our portions (this term eyedrop had also become a standard unit of measure in villages after our Great Leader instituted the lowered-rations policy).

With eyes accustomed to making sure I wasn't being cheated, I sized up the half portion of fish paste allocated to my bowl. I had to admit that the error was on the order of no more than one or two parts in ten thousand.

Men who could share a single bowl of food in the camps were men who were capable of being friends to the death. Many years later, when I tasted the pleasure of sex for the first time, I thought back to the enjoyment of this meal together. Stealing things or going against the system by buying something from a neighbouring villager, then by lucky fluke getting it into the Number, cooking it and, after cooking, splitting it evenly so that when we ate the first bite we had the same overwhelming feeling of gladness – this was something that a single person could not experience. Both the physicality of it and the high degree of psychological satisfaction can be compared to sexual union.

I am not a homosexual and I believe that there were very few homosexuals among the convicts, but this intense experience was similar to having had sex together. It would be inaccurate to use the word friendship to describe the relationship.

On what basis was friendship or this state beyond friendship established? Similar tastes? Eating! Mutual interests? Eating! The same aspirations? Eating! The same habits? Stealing things to eat! Similar character? Having an insatiable desire to eat! Eat, eat, eat! No matter how well-bred or slovenly the person, whether he was well educated or poorly educated or had no education at all, whether he was a political convict or a criminal convict, in this regard every person was the same. If you were to say that this relationship was 'friendship' then all the convicts would be quite compatible.

The politically created famine returned every person to his original biological state so that the only things left were the two primary functions of eating and having sex. After the sex ability had withered, due to hunger and malnourishment, all that was left to indicate that here was a living being was eating. And so, when one convict and another stole, cooked, divided the meal and ate together, any latent sexuality not completely obliterated would revive to a minuscule degree ... and the reproductive organ would stir ever so slightly. Satisfaction of the appetite and sexual satisfaction are strangely connected. Back then, if you had eaten well, you could simply say that you had enjoyed an orgasm.

Relations within the same sex were this way; relations between sexes were even more so. Love or perhaps the sexual urge seemed to be stronger in the physical make-up of women than in men, and in the worst famine it could not be extinguished. If a female convict happened to fall in love with a male convict, or if a wife working in the same camp wanted to express her concern for her convict husband, she would save back food for him. She'd put a remaining bit of steamed bun in her pocket so that when she had an opportunity to be working near her man she could slip over when the Troop Leader wasn't looking and tuck the treasure into his clothes or shoes at the edge of the field.

After work, putting on his shoes again the man would find this bit of food still warm from the woman's loving body. He would immediately stuff it in his mouth. But as he chewed and swallowed, a feeling akin to the satisfaction of sex would well up in his body. For the female, this success and the feeling of gladness at being able to give her man some food would be the same as if she had flung off her clothes and lain naked in the grass, waiting for him to stroke and caress her. If she was fortunate enough to see him in the distance gnawing on the bun, her lower regions would become moist. The cruelest reality cannot extinguish the most beautiful things in the world.

And so, after thinking again about my relationship with Heh, I have concluded that it may be appropriate and accurate to describe our feelings as homosexual love. As for how food and sex are related in the physiology of a person, and how the various layers of the psyche are involved, these things are better left to a psychologist to analyse. I only want to say here that when I was alerted to the fact that this new convict wanted to turn in Heh Deng, I truly felt extreme concern.

Exposing people is like a fad. If you don't do it when you should you are contravening the fashion. It is as though men are all wearing pants and you are contrary enough to wear a skirt. Moreover, if you don't defend in moral terms why you differ from others, then you are likely to be regarded as a freak and treated as one. Exposing people is also one of the beneficial activities greatly encouraged and praised by leaders and masses alike. Exposing people is considered to be saving them, delivering them from evil – why not encourage a virtuous and courageous man to save a drowning person!

The reason I am not willing to accuse others is that I am a coward. I can't stand to watch someone I have exposed receive certain kinds of punishment. Also, as soon as I think that there might be a chance the accused will confront me to my face, I lose courage. I don't consider myself better than others because of this. I have been living in this social environment since my youth, since the year 1949 – it is impossible for me to make any moral judgements about those who inform on others.

The Great Cultural Revolution erupted several years after this diary was written. It produced a new slogan: 'Noisily make revolution in the deepest dark places of your soul!' The dark recesses of my soul were alarmed on hearing that phrase. I realized that for years, since 1949, a kind of terror had infiltrated those hidden places in people's souls. This encroaching terror turned out to be far stronger than sexual relationships, or blood ties, or any of mankind's most intimate relations between homosexuals, man and wife, father and son. All those came to be capable of informing on and exposing each other. Leaders were constantly exhorting people to be courageous in turning others in. Was it courage or was it terror that made them do so?

And so, when I heard Troop Leader Zheng say, 'This is just the start ... there will be others,' I knew that I would have to report on Heh. Since I was relatively familiar with him, it appeared quite reasonable that I should draw a clear line between us, and so I prepared to make a statement. I still remember with great clarity how I sat with my legs crossed on the edge of the kang, making my notes, first in the dusk of evening and then under the flickering light of an oil lamp. I sat on a ragged bedcover surrounded by the stares of the others. There was nowhere to hide, no way to shirk the task. Troop Leader Zheng had assigned me as note-taker for the meeting on Heh Deng's affairs, which was a clear

73

signal. 'There'll be others.' Who? Me! The hand holding the pen began to shake with fear, yet I had to summon up courage as I made the decision to write an accusatory report. Was it courage or was it terror? I can't say for sure.

16 September

When it was time for breakfast in the morning Su Qin dawdled, made everyone upset. Then he forgot the door wasn't locked until we had already reached the work site, so was criticized by Group Leader Chen. Su confronted Chen and said, 'I can't be Group Leader!'

Went today to Canal Sixteen to harvest sunflower seeds. Before starting work, Chen photographed Zhou in front of everyone, wanted everyone to keep him under surveillance. Zhou was embarrassed and angry, yelled as he knelt on the ground, 'Bastard! I haven't done anything and he has everyone stare at me! I won't put up with it! I'd rather go and cut rice.' In the end he left with Group Leader Chen; don't know what work Chen made him do.

Morning cut sunflower stalks with Bai Jizu. Bai said he had Ma Weixiao get guest rations for him, after four extra helpings he still wasn't full. Study session in the evening – we exposed Heh. I made a statement. In addition to criticizing him I added some other things.

Zhou got lucky today, bought two kuai worth of chicken eggs, but he wrote a self-criticism too.

New arrivals were gossiping today, said demands on cadres on the Outside very severe, any problem at all and you were sent in to labour reform.

17 September

Today continued the work of yesterday. Su Qin conducted the work assignment in the morning and it was a mess. It takes ability to assign work for over twenty men in a short time.

Heh sick today, probably due to his mood. Troop Leader Zheng looked after him in a sense by letting him rest for the day.

18 September

Morning to Farm Canal Eighteen to harvest sunflower seeds. Chen Lin said there were still a lot of people eating greens in Group Seventeen; as a result we were transferred back to hauling rice stalks. The harvesting, binding, transporting of rice this year a big problem; half the water wouldn't drain in half the fields.

A number of people guessed it was Liu Xiangru and Long

Zhengang telling on the greens-eaters. I don't think that could be. A lot of people are doing bad things themselves yet they go around reporting on others.

19 September

Rumour yesterday that we would be allowed to rest today. Indeed, today is a rest day. Morning Group Leader Zheng wanted me to write material exposing Heh Deng. Before I'd written more than a few words there was a big meeting to reorganize the groups.

People in our Small Group are all being sent to other places. Heh, Zhou, Ma, Bai are being transferred to Station Three, two hundred convicts altogether.

I'm still at Headquarters, still in Group Seventeen, but except for me everyone is new. One named Tan says he knows my name, read poems I published, is very friendly towards me.

Our new Group Seventeen not too strong. Group Leader Wang Sanyu is an old Sick Number. In this group I'm not as good as the best but am still a long way from the worst.

At three in the afternoon all the convicts of the whole camp held an Autumn Harvest Mobilization meeting. Station Leader Yan announced the target quotas we had to meet for the harvest. Cutting: each day one mou two fen. Binding stalks: two mou.

Transporting: every person has to back-haul a distance of no less than sixty hua-li and to carry no less than eighty jin on their backs per trip. After Station Leader Yan finished, Camp Leader Wen made a speech severely criticizing negative work habits, running off, and other kinds of bad behaviour. According to him, Troop Leader Kang was corrupt only to the extent of twenty-some yuan, but was sentenced to seven years. Now they say that if you make fewer than a dozen bricks a day you can be sentenced to seven or eight years – and no need for a court of law to be involved. Convicts scared shitless by this information. Camp Leader Wen also mentioned that from today onward we would be divided by class to eat. Now this is something that merits some thought!

After the meeting, the new Group Leader Wang Sanyu drafted a copy of the Small Group's Performance Guarantee. By the looks of him Wang is not too plebeian, unlike other Group Leaders who can only shout slogans. For example, he proposed that we oppose low tastes and oppose talking only about eating and drinking; instead we should read books and newspapers.

*T*oday, in China, people appear to want to forget the past. Ours is a collective past, and many feel that parts of our common heritage are best left alone.

Back then, labour reform camps were set up throughout China and the fates of all Chinese had a certain similarity to them. So many experienced the same fate that there was no point in talking about it. Anyone's specific pain was anchored by a more general pain. In evaluating what one had been through, a measure of individual shock had already been dissipated. The proverb 'there are people beyond the people, there is more heaven beyond the heavens' was endowed with a new meaning in China – there was vast trauma behind one's own little trauma.

Do people, then, really need to have that period of history revisited once again? Does a description of the reality of that time have any relevance today?

It is impossible for me not to ask this question, and not to care about the answer. I find it hard to believe that what terrifies me to this day, what often jolts me out of my sleep, can disappear from the world's consciousness as easily as a passing breeze.

Yet I sense with apprehension that readers now seem more interested in fantasy than the reality of what happened, and happened quite recently. Perhaps history tinted and repainted is more interesting than straight narration of real events. But there are profound implications in this unwillingness to face the recent past.

One issue, of course, is simply the ability to remember, to recognize the brutal limitations we all accepted on how we could think. As the wounds heal over, we are unable to recall how our minds worked back then. In terms of literary style, the people in this book all seem like caricatures. This contravenes a guiding principle long followed in Chinese literature that calls for detailed description of character. The thinness of the stick figures in this historical record should not be blamed on inadequate character portrayal, however. When a social environment violently eradicates anything that appears unique to an individual, scrapes away everything related to culture, when it returns a person to his most basic animal condition, his life and death can only be portrayed in the crudest of strokes. The labour camps in China in 1960 were an ideal laboratory for those wanting to understand the fundamentals of man's nature. They were not ideal for providing material for literary subtleties.

The former Soviet Union and Eastern Europe have published a number of descriptions of life in labour camps during and after the Stalinist period. I have read all that I could find with great respect. Readers of this book may find that in some ways China's camps and the Soviet Union's camps were similar, but readers may also begin to discern some differences. This book does not intend to draw comparisons or conclusions. In narrating events, the profundity is in the precision of the details. If absolutely accurate, the book achieves its required depth. Universality does not come from evaluations an author makes later.

If my point had been to make a general conclusion about that period in China, or about labour camps in general, not only would this book be superfluous, it would be positively harmful. In order to write these notations I have revisited as exhaustively as possible things that I experienced directly. I have excised any information that came later and that may have influenced my thinking. I have tried to record accurately the passage of one individual. This book may not have a great deal of literary value, but I sincerely hope it will provide a measure of sociological and psychological insight. From this raw material, I hope we may begin to glean some information about where our future may be headed.

There are many reasons that Chinese, and intellectuals in particular, are not inclined to revisit and analyse their own pasts. As members of the socio-psycho-political entity called Chinese society, we were embedded in a complex web of fears, hopes and motivations. A close examination will show that China's labour camps possessed peculiarities that are characteristic of the Chinese people in general. For instance, in the course of my twenty-two-year career in the camps, I rarely encountered convicts who did not cooperate with the system and with prison authorities from the start. There were very few who felt hatred or resentment about being a political prisoner, or even about being a 'wrongly judged case'.

This was especially true among intellectuals. There were many political prisoners among the convicts, but few of them had a clearly defined political agenda or point of view. They certainly did not represent the perspective of earlier political currents in China. For example, they lacked the vigour of those who followed immediately after the May Fourth Movement [1919], men and women who promoted an awareness of democracy and human rights. On the contrary, what the few who were politically inclined represented was a corrupt and outdated regime, a regime that in theoretical, political and military terms was defunct.

The behaviour of this kind of convict in the camp made people despise them even more than a normal criminal convict. These people did not go around espousing anti-communist propaganda, a handle that would immediately have been grabbed onto in lifestyle examination meetings. Rather they bragged about their 'stinking' former lifestyles in order to prove that people were not as well off today as they had been before, that people in the new society were not as happy as in the old society.

These men were not remotely capable of being recognized by the convicts around them as having that historically revered status of political prisoner. On the contrary, they made others feel that it was imperative that they be reformed. 'What will happen to us if these dregs of society are not reformed!' They served as a perfect example for the opposition – labour reform authorities often used them in their speeches as confirmation that anti-government activity leads necessarily to a decline in morals. Other convicts took this to heart as an object lesson, making them even more vigilant in accomplishing their own self-reform.

As for the great majority of intellectual convicts, they carried a sense of guilt for the original crime that they may or may not have committed, as well as guilt for newly discovered crimes for which they were now painstakingly reforming themselves. This great majority, I must say, included me. You will find no precedent in any history book of prison authorities and prisoners having such an intimate symbiosis. Some convicts would even design their own methods of self-reform, such as voluntarily 'sweeping clean the obstacles on the road to Thought Reform'. An example would be that zealot who brought a case against Troop Leader Ma.

In terms of what we now call psychology, this was a bizarre period. I doubt we will ever see such a Golden Age of Thought Reform played out again. Naturally there was behaviour that didn't conform to the wishes of the camp authorities, such as running away, stealing, eating greens, playing dead-dog, loafing on the job, etc. But these were incipient cracks between body and soul that were as likely to occur in a normal person as in an intellectual. The flesh had been tormented to hell and back, so that sometimes it had no alternative but to indulge in some bad practice. The main point was that in most intellectual convicts the spirit was still devoted to the cause. Among the torments visited upon intellectuals in the camps, therefore, was self-castigation. When criminal convicts did bad things, the impulse issued purely from physical need. There was no attendant compulsion to fret. When intellectuals did bad things on account of physical need, however, even if they weren't found out they would begin to feel depraved. They would live in fear of moral decline.

Another phenomenon peculiar to Chinese labour reform camps related to the leadership style of the authorities. Almost all the leaders with whom I had direct contact stood before us as the heads of one large family. A familial sense of concern accompanied their severity. No matter how absurd the lesson they might be administering, or how bitterly painful the method of reform, we had the vague impression that someone was warmly caring for us even as we endured the physical and mental trauma. The Old Commissar and the Camp

Leaders always put it this way: 'We really can't stand it if we're not able to turn your iron into steel!' Convicts driven almost to the point of death could be made to feel ashamed of themselves.

There is no sense of sarcasm here, or desire to put something over on my readers. It really was that way, and it felt completely natural to be that way. In fact, I still feel this sense of familial responsibility. No matter how absurd or how intense the criticism of me, if I can see through to a beneficent motive hidden behind the words, and if those words are wrapped in the spirit of 'I'm doing this for your own good', then I can't help but feel that I have disappointed the hopes for me held by other members of the family. I feel I have taken a wrong fork in the road.

I believe that a kind of collective subconscious had penetrated the minds of everyone in the country some thirty-five years ago. I say it was a collective subconscious because this kind of awareness manifested itself not only among the convicts but also among the labour reform authorities. My personal experience makes me believe that, while the authorities (in concrete terms, let us say the Old Commissar) regarded us as enemies, we were also children who could be taught to mend our ways. As soon as someone behaved 'well', was a 'good child', the rudimentary humanity of the authorities would build upon this concept of everyone's being a member of a larger household.

Camp leaders were not following any public security rules or stringent camp laws in governing us. Camp rules and laws were like all the other rules and laws in China – they were abstract, general principles fundamentally lacking any specifics that one could point to as an example. Laws had no consistent interpretation, and so there was no knowing how one should execute them. The corollary was that those in power could, with impunity, execute laws according to their own interpretation.

We were, therefore, governed by the grim whimsy of a paternalistic system. At times the mental state of our 'fathers' approached aberrant behaviour, or even madness (severe whipping, for instance, or using terrible ways of 'photographing'* a convict). That was the prerogative of a mad head of the family. The reason our entire flawed system managed to function, however, was precisely because it was supported by traditional family practices that had never been written down as laws. As the saying goes, the robe of the sky is seamless, and it is often the unwritten laws that are most important.

For example, the labour reform authorities would secretly adopt a lenient attitude towards a convict whose 'wrongly decided' status was absolutely clear. A well-treated convict might, as a result, find that life was far easier in the camps than it would be on the Outside. Of course at that time all convicts had wrongly decided cases – the distinctions lay in those that were obvious and those that were not so obvious. I, for example, was a convict whose miscarriage of justice was not at all obvious since my published poetry was there for all to see, in black characters on white paper. Moreover, my poetry was known to have exerted a pernicious negative influence on society.

Mao Zedong said, 'Without distinctions there is no

---

* Various ways of singling one person out for public scrutiny and ridicule.

policy.' Without distinction, society took large numbers of innocent people and sent them into the camps to do forced labour – but in the camps they were then assigned new distinctions. Convicts who were obviously crimeless were to be considered high-class convicts. This seemed to remedy the errors in social policies, allowing them to be more perfectly executed. In a period when the entire population of China was experiencing famine, quite a few high-class convicts lived to return home only to discover that all the members of their families had died of starvation. In a properly administered country they, too, I fear, would have perished.

A system of law does not make decisions based on sentiment, whereas in our lawless country family sentiments were what prevailed. Severe and often prejudicial policies were ameliorated by the invisible hand of ancient traditions. The result was fair enough and balanced enough that many people were able to stay alive and were even happy to go on living under the system. The same is true today. Whether this is rational and understandable or not, such has been my personal observation.

Heh Deng was criticized and struggled against several times, and then was stripped of his responsibility as Group Leader. His replacement was Su Qin. This man was not remotely like his namesake, the famous political strategist of the Warring States period who was so well versed in disputation. The moment our Su Qin opened his mouth to speak, the spit flew in all directions. He used hands and feet to supplement the deficiencies of his words so that he seemed forever to be in a state of crisis.

He had been a middle-school teacher before, although who knows how he lectured his students. From the few speeches he gave us, squeezed out of him by the Troop Leader in our study sessions and lifestyle-examination meetings, his thinking was as confused and twisted as a ball of string. It was useless for us to wait for anything rational to come from his lips. What's more, everything he said revolved around the subject of eating. Although this was certainly an enduring topic, much as love is to literature, it was sometimes inappropriate in the formal setting of labour reform camp meetings. Especially when the Troop Leader made an august appearance, convicts were expected to talk about the greater truth of politics. They were to make every effort to show how well they had been reforming themselves. Su Qin, perversely, would not play along. From the moment he entered the camp, he seemed to have cast off politics without the slightest regard for the impression he made on others.

He wore spectacles with lenses like bottle bottoms for near-sightedness – this showed that he was an intellectual who had received a certain education. But behind those two round rings of glass his goldfish eyes were perpetually focused on the food bucket. Earlier, when divvying up food was still handled at the Small Group level, he could be more critical than a criminal convict about the person wielding the ladle. At each meal he would make a huge fuss, sometimes even snatching the bowl of someone he thought had got a little more. And while he snatched, he shouted. Yellow spit would be flying everywhere, to the extent that every one of us knew what it tasted like.

The entire group found him odious. On 5 August I was obliged to write a big-character poster against him, saying that he had a certain deviousness with regard to the question of food (as though I was not devious at all). I added a few political slogans as wrapping paper around the main theme. As they say, 'When the wall is about to collapse, everybody gives it a push,' and he had clearly reached this stage.

He had one excellent attribute, however: no matter how others criticized or wrote big-character posters against him, it was as though he had his ear to the wind. He heard nothing, he never harboured a grudge, he just stuck single-mindedly to his focus on food. (This kind of intellectual was bound to survive. If he ever reads this narration of what happened in the past, I ask him to forgive me. I am only describing as truthfully as possible the effect he had at that time on others.) His appearance was certainly not very refined, but who was good-looking back then? And yet he doggedly went out to work every day, back bent as he scurried before the line of men like a monkey.

I say like a monkey because he was nimble and his head and body were small. Such a small person ate exactly the same ration of food as I did, so how could I possibly not be jealous of him? This, too, was a reason that I, who was generally unwilling to write large-character posters, specifically chose him as someone from whom to earn merit points.

It was amazing that our leaders would appoint this man as head of our group. Leaders have their own way of looking at things, though, and later I, too, came to understand. Su Qin was a 'clearly wrong convict' – his was an obvious case of having no crime. He never talked about this and he never complained of being wronged; he seemed to have come into the camps purely for the sake of looking for something to eat. The leaders considered this one trait alone an incomparable virtue. No matter how he antagonized other convicts, or how they criticized him, the leaders seemed to have decided on him from the start. Although he did not enjoy any more freedom as Small Group Leader, he was to a degree treated as a high-class convict.

His exclusive concentration on getting enough to eat meant that he neglected his duties, though, to the extent that he forgot the leaders had made an exception in promoting him to Small Group Leader. On the second day of his new job he got out of bed as usual and squatted on his bunk hugging his knees, bowl in hand, waiting for someone else to call him to eat. The rest of the group had already come to think of him as Small Group Leader; Heh Deng naturally could not take back his old job so he, too, sat there fuming. The entire group simply held their bowls and waited. Not until people passed by our window on their way back to their Numbers, stirring hot gruel as they went, did Su Qin suddenly wake up to the fact that he was supposed to call us to eat. He scrambled up, stretched out his neck like a goose, and shouted 'Food!'

The gruel in the wooden bucket had turned to little but water. This was the first count against Su Qin, something that annoyed everyone.

The second was that we arrived at the workplace before he remembered the door had not been locked. Locking the door of the Number was one of the Small

Group Leader's main responsibilities. In an official labour reform camp, which ours was not, the lock on the door of a Number and the key were under the supervision of the police. It was probably this one point that distinguished us as being different from an official camp. Guards with guns policed the outer perimeter of our main headquarters, but inside each unit within that larger enclosure surveillance was the responsibility of Troop Leaders and Small Group Leaders selected from among the ranks of convicts. It is a proven fact that this method of control is more effective than forceful supervision with bayonets and guns. The nerve endings of camp authorities did not have to, and indeed were unable to, extend to every corner of every Number.

Usually if a sick convict stayed at home on a given day, it was his responsibility to watch over everyone's belongings. It was best, of course, to have two sick convicts so that they would keep watch over each other. If either wanted to steal things it had to be done from some other Number. If the sick convict happened to be a perennial thief or criminal convict, he would be handed over to the Troop Leader at the start of the day, who would gather together all such misfits and assign them to do some light task. Only a high-class convict was ever allowed the luxury of staying alone in a Number, lying on the bunk and basking in solitude. (I was given such an opportunity once, although I used the chance to run off to the fields to eat watermelon.)

It happened that nobody had been left at home as a sick convict on this day. Everyone had come to the fields to cut sunflower stalks. The first to become concerned about whether or not the Number's door had been locked was a convict whose family had sent him things to eat. He asked Su Qin, whose face went blank before realizing that he had not performed his duties properly. Several of the relatively rich convicts now pointed at him and began to shout.

'Bastard! You don't even lock the door. What kind of asshole Small Group Leader are you?'

'Who's going to be responsible when we lose things? Can you make it up to us?'

Convicts with nothing worth stealing grabbed the chance to join in, scythes in hand, in order to rest for a while. Big Group Leader Chen Lin also felt that this was a fairly serious matter. If the door was unlocked he was bound to have innumerable cases of unresolvable petty thievery on his hands.

A number of petty thieves in the labour camp have been described above. They were divided into three types. The first stole only things that were publicly owned – people who ate greens were included in this category and it can be safely said that every convict was guilty of this. I belonged to this first category.

Stealing public property was not called 'stealing' but rather 'taking'. The experts in this category not only were not disliked by others, but enjoyed their general respect. One member of a travelling theatre group who had committed the crime of male-female relations was actually able to get up on the roof of the big kitchen during Spring Festival. From the window he let down a thin wire with a steel hook on the end, and, as though fishing, caught himself several of the flatbreads that the cook had been making for the Troop Leaders. He was apprehended only because he ate too many and was unable to crawl back down again. He lay on the roof until it was light and the cooks came along and discovered him. When they pulled him down his body was covered with a layer of white frost and his hands and feet were frozen stiff. After the cooks beat him up, the Troop Leaders, painfully regretting the loss of their holiday pancakes, locked him in solitary confinement for one week.

When they opened the door, he emerged a hero, a person with high standing in the camp. Later, he imperceptibly became General Consultant to all the petty thieves and it was said that he forbade them from stealing people's private belongings. He insisted that they take only public property. Still later it was said that a female convict fell in love with him and swore that she would marry no one else. But that is another story.

The second category of thief did not make any distinctions about whether something was publicly or privately owned. Anything they saw was fair game. Although these people could find edibles wherever they went, and were often successful thieves, they were also the most easily apprehended. If they were found out they were not treated lightly – if the rat crossed the street in daylight it got beaten by everyone.

If you had been caught once as a number-two category of thief, you were henceforth called a 'numbered dead dog'. From the Troop Leaders down to the convict with the fewest belongings, everyone scrutinized your activities. If anyone lost anything, people would turn on you first.

Criminal convicts were not the only ones shameless enough to steal others' food. I have witnessed the corrupting effect that starvation has on a person. If an intellectual convict fell into the situation of not being able to put his hands on enough to eat, he would first start by taking public property – eating greens. If nothing held him from going further, he would begin to steal at random. Toads hopping on the ground, cabbages in the field, biscuits in convicts' personal wooden boxes – there was no owner's tag on any of these saying that they were private property. How could famished eyes that glowed red with hunger distinguish subtle lines between public and private? If a starving intellectual stole someone else's property and got away with it, he would quickly begin to lose any upbringing and education he once had and would repeatedly choose this most convenient way of staying alive. Satisfying hunger is supremely real and matter-of-fact. Abstract moral concepts are blown aside when one is facing the dividing line between life and death.

This was particularly so since intellectuals had already confessed that they had committed some crime or other. They had already voluntarily relinquished to the leaders their self-respect and self-confidence. Having surrendered these two psychological weapons of self-defence, the next step was simple. The difference between 'criminal' and 'dead dog' was not very great. Already a criminal, what did it matter if one was also a dead dog – it seemed to be fifty steps making fun of one hundred steps. Who gives a damn – first survive and then think about it!

Who could have known, though, that the habit of stealing, condemned by mankind since the dawn of history, can easily develop into a habit like taking drugs? It only takes one small hole for the dam of ethical conduct to crumble for good. I am not saying that these intellectuals would necessarily continue to steal after leaving the camps, but that they were infected with an attitude of disdain for ethical conduct. This attitude, though invisible, continues to have a powerful effect on the way they live their lives.

By now, the fact of a starving population is a thing of the past, but I have seen the scars of famine on a number of intellectuals who came through that terrifying period. They might be regarded as eminent scholars and gentlemen today, but even as they give lofty speeches and write highbrow opinions, under their cheap Western suits I can detect a thieving third hand.

The third category was that of professional part-time thieves. These men would puff themselves up with righteousness if they were accused of doing anything wrong. If something was missing they would even help everyone look for it. This sort of thief was invariably a free convict or a high-class convict, someone who had the opportunity to roam at will in the camp yard after the troops had gone to work. They wouldn't dare break into a locked Number – that was too obvious. But if the door wasn't locked and there was no convict inside keeping watch, this was their target. They would not limit themselves to stealing things to eat. Since their tastes were similar to people on the Outside, different from people facing imminent starvation, they would steal anything that might be worth any money. For example, they would take a pen, something considered worthless by men on the Inside. Imagine trying to establish a case against this kind of thief!

When something went missing in a Small Group, the one who had been robbed was not the only one who suffered. The event represented a calamity to the Small Group Leader and Big Group Leader. Although the authorities were not concerned about the material possessions of convicts, an increase in the number of thefts threatened order in the camps as well as the mood of convicts reforming inside them. This was something that could not be ignored. When a thief could not be found, the ire of the authorities had to land somewhere – Troop Leaders and the Camp Leader would hold the Small and Large Group Leaders responsible. They were substitutes for the thief in taking the punishment.

This was why Chen Lin was now quite upset, and why he pointed at Su Qin's nose as he shouted, 'What do you do to earn your food? You don't even know enough to lock the door! You motherfucker, you spend all day staring at your rice bowl, that bowl is more important to you than your fucking old lady!'

Chen Lin had been a newspaper reporter. He was not a vulgar person, and would come out with this kind of language only if pushed to extremity. Yet when he described Su Qin's degree of respect for his rice bowl he was being quite accurate. Having lost the ability and desire for sex, most of us would not have thought of juxtaposing Su Qin's regard for his bowl with a normal man's regard for his wife. The sunflower field was soon echoing with laughter as we realized how appropriate this analogy was.

Quite unexpectedly, Su Qin confronted Chen Lin. He threw down the scythe in his hand. The glare from his bulging yellow goldfish eyes pierced the thick glasses as he said, 'I quit! I'm not up to being Group Leader. Tell the Troop Leader to choose someone else. Hell, you don't even get more to eat if you're Group Leader!'

It was true that a Small Group Leader's regular rations were no greater than the rations of the members of his Group.

This was the only case of refusing an appointment I ever saw in the labour camps. Most who wanted to be Group Leader were not allowed to be. I felt as though I had just witnessed an act of courage. Su Qin's back no longer seemed stooped and I could not help but feel respect for him. At the same time I was ashamed of myself. Here I was constantly afraid of this or that, anxious about getting something and then about losing it. I both wanted to steal greens and at the same time wanted to keep face. As I continued to steal greens, I continued writing poems lauding the leaders of the camp and their new dialectic. I wanted desperately to achieve the status of high-class convict.

Troop Leader Zheng had rebuked me by saying that I was involved with everything bad that went on. He also put me in the ranks of the most serious offenders of eating greens. On the other hand, I was still fretting in the diary that 'under conditions of scarcity, people's relations with one another became abnormal and callous, relationships of naked economic profit'. Moreover, my own conscience made me work to control myself. I took seriously the various means of reforming people in the camps: lifestyle-examination meetings, study sessions, criticism and praise meetings, awards for meritorious actions, etc.

For example: 'Evening judged who should be given awards for meritorious service. A list of people to be praised, everybody snickered, not at all respectful.' Here I was expressing distaste for other people's behaviour. Clearly I felt that those awards deserved serious consideration.

In short, I was unable to see through to the heart of the matter as clearly as Su Qin did. I was unable to grasp the fundamentals of life and cling to that understanding as the unbreakable thread that would carry me through. As a result I developed a number of inappropriate concerns.

Zhou was another example of someone whose mind was extremely clear. Once he found and cooked a mangled rabbit leg that had been left behind by a hawk. He was the one who should have been considered the most serious offender of eating greens, not I; and so when Troop Leader Zheng singled me out I felt victimized. From the diary it can be seen that hardly a day went by in which Zhou did not steal something to eat. When the Big Group Leader criticized him, however, Zhou dared to point out that the Big Group Leader himself was taking double orders of food, stealing watermelon, and so on.

When the Troop Leader came to have a word with him, he countered by asking, 'Why is it some are so fat and yet some are so thin?' The questions with the easiest answers are often those least easily answered – Zhou dared to use this kind of dangerous reactionary talk to criticize the Troop Leader.

On the morning when Su Qin cast off his black gauze hat, that is, his official post, Chen Lin dragged Zhou out of the line of men before we started to work and told him to stand in front of us to be photographed. This was the most gentle means of punishment and was really no more than a pre-emptive warning. In the eyes of most convicts it was not punishment at all, but even this made Zhou violently angry. 'I haven't done a thing and he has everyone look at me! I won't put up with it! I'd rather go cut rice!' Like Su Qin, he despised the hierarchical structure of the labour reform camp authorities and the system of rules; instead of complying he simply squatted on the ground and refused to get up.

In the end neither Su Qin nor Zhou was given any punishment at all. After Su Qin voluntarily quit his post, he cut down a large sunflower head and put it between his legs like a monkey; then one by one popped sunflower seeds husk and all into his mouth. The spit flew from the corners of his lips as he chewed. Chen Lin couldn't figure out what to do about this, so he switched focus and ordered Zhou to get up and follow him.

'Dogshitter! If you want to cut rice, I'll let you cut rice!' he said. Harvesting rice was much harder work than cutting sunflower stalks. That year half the water in the rice fields wouldn't drain. A person had to bend over and wade through deep muck, which could be considered a form of punishment in itself. But after Zhou went off with Chen Lin, who knows what negotiations took place – not only did he not have to harvest rice but he came home that evening as happy as could be, carrying four chicken eggs and claiming that he had spent two yuan to buy them.

Zhou was also a convict with a clear-cut case of misjustice. Although he repeatedly contravened the rules of the camps, before long he was transferred to the envied and prestigious position of doctor in the infirmary. He was wearing a white coat, and a stethoscope hung from his neck when I went in to be examined. He sat behind a desk, very much in the manner of a doctor. 'What's the problem? Hunger! Go back and work harder.' He said this in his Sichuan accent with great relish. It was impossible to tell that he was still a convict who despised the labour reform system and who still had some resistance left in him. He gave me no medicine except ferrous sulphate; he certainly did not grant me a day of rest. We had been together in the same group too long – no matter how well I performed there was no fooling him. He was now even better than the Troop Leader at protecting the interests of the labour camp authorities.

It can be said that all men plucked out from our ranks to be high-class convicts shared feelings of superiority. (Why else should I struggle so hard to become a high-class convict?) It didn't matter that privately these men still considered themselves to be wrongly judged. This was because the final result of a wrongly judged case was getting unequal and better treatment so that injustices in society were evened out upon entering the labour reform camp. Everyone knew that times were hard on the Outside, even harder perhaps than inside the camps; so that to be a high-class convict was equivalent to ducking into an alley that protected you from the wind.

Entries for September in the diary confirm this. 'Today heard new arrivals talking, saying that right now on the Outside the demands on cadres are very strict – any problem at all and they are sent in for labour reform.' 'Camp Leader Wen reported that Troop Leader Kang was corrupt to the extent of twenty-some yuan, and for that he was sentenced to seven years.' 'Right now a man could be sentenced to seven or eight years based on nothing more than the rule about making at least twelve bricks – and there was no need for any court to consider the case.'

Who would want to go back into an Outside world like that? Who would want to enjoy that kind of treatment as a free civilian? To be sentenced for not completing a convict's work quota! It was enough to make even convicts bury their heads in fear. This was not using the threat of prison to terrify free civilians, but using the desperation of free civilians to terrify convicts.

Comparing Inside and Outside, it seemed better to stay in the camps. Chinese have long believed that poverty is bearable but unequal treatment is not. When those governing us so equitably brought enormous pressure to bear on each person, each felt only the warmth and blessing of that equal treatment and did not take issue with the degree of pressure. This is probably a key reason political manipulation of the people could continue and even flourish in the 1960s.

Often all the effort one put into being good was in vain. Struggling against others, exposing others, judging relative merit, zealously making public statements, reforming yourself by meekly putting your head down and doing hard labour ... yet as soon as groups were reorganized you had to start all over again. You were separated from the people you had been with before, so all the accumulated merit as well as the accumulated mistakes went back to zero.

By 18 September, for several days and nights we had held numerous criticism-and-struggle sessions against Heh Deng. Since Heh Deng was someone with whom I had eaten from the same pot, someone who had covered for me when I cheated with the measuring stick, someone with whom I shared a very strong bond, I was conscientiously trying to figure out how to save myself without at the same time bringing him physical harm. Just then the labour reform troops held a big meeting to announce a reorganization.

Given the way things are now in China, this all seems like a surreal kind of shadow play. The moral dilemma about Heh was so overwhelming, and so tormented my young soul, that I was utterly consumed by it at the time. Yet later it became no more substantial than the air. It was a forgotten trifle, a puff of wind.

There are things that do not allow even for the trace of memories. I feel there is no remaining scar on my psyche of the terror and pain of that time. None the less, many extremely conscientious people died in that trifling matter. And they died most conscientiously. There were several thousand people doing labour reform together with me, and of these roughly one-third died. Although one could often rationalize that criticism could be couched in a way that enabled both to live, in all too many cases, it was 'You die, or I die.'

A sudden reorganization of the troop was meant to be a surprise attack against the possibility of convicts forming solidarity groups; it was also intended to regroup convicts of a particular type according to the camp's work needs. The first purpose revealed how little the authorities understood the psychology of convicts. Although their tentacles tried to reach into every little crevice there was still a great gulf between them and us. The fact of the matter was that the men were so hungry it was fundamentally impossible for them to band together in gangs.

Reorganization was not totally bad. Both the accomplishments and the mistakes of the past could disappear in the wake of the changes and convicts could start fresh under brand-new terms. We could be born again, we could start a new day!

What were these fresh new days like? Read on.

20 September

Morning went to Canal Nine to harvest rice. Couldn't pull my legs out of the mud. Tried hard all morning, kept at it, exhausted. Dizzy by noon, but nothing I could do. Han Dianming saved a few leftovers from breakfast and asked who wanted them – was immediately surrounded by three or four people. Yu Guozhen and Shu Geng were about to fight over it and just grab. I was going to ask for some but decided to forget it when I saw the situation.

New arrivals like Jin, Han, Li don't work too badly. Don't know how long they can keep it up though.

Very depressed because so tired. No hope of graduating this year, no chance of any improvement in living conditions. Mother's hopes for my future; getting older . . . year after year here has nothing in it of value. Escaping is for fools and am not strong enough to try to get ahead by sheer labour – if I put out even a little effort my heart begins to pound.

Qu wanted to eat Han's leftovers, put a lot into convincing him, said inappropriate things like he would get him medicine, calories, etc.

Afternoon they looked after our group, allowed us to gather fallen rice stalks. At evening study group discussed work efficiency.

21 September

Went to Canal Ten to harvest rice. Yu Guozhen wouldn't go in the water. Lin yelled that he was going to drag him in. They're going to cut his food ration again; he fought and argued all morning.

At noon, finishing work, every person had to carry rice stalks. Troop Leader Zheng thought I carried too few, took me and some others to the bank of the canal to be photographed. Used his rope to single me out, saying, 'Why is it you're involved with everything bad?' With my body like this, what else can I do? As a result not allowed to rest at noon, had to back-haul more. Evening very late before we stopped working.

Putting us old-timers and new arrivals together is going to do us in; utterly worn out these days.

22 September

Again to Canal Ten to finish the work there. I served as man on duty so had to carry water. Very embarrassed but asked Han Dianming if I could have some of his leftover food. Must find some way to control desire to eat! Afternoon transferred rice stalks up onto the banks of the paddy field. Troop Leader Zheng again resented our working so slowly, again assigned us to haul stalks on our backs. Hauled three trips. Stopped work very late that night, ate, then listened to Camp Leader Bai's report. He read out sixteen names of people eligible for graduation. Asked everyone to discuss. Chen Lin was among them.

23 September

Canal Two harvested rice stalks. Group Seventeen always being criticized, giving very bad impression to the leaders. Putting old and weak and sick members together with new arrivals is not the way – it's going to finish us off.

24 September

Canal Two harvested rice stalks. Group Seventeen again criticized. Cannot satisfy superiors. Do the leaders know the conditions in Group Seventeen? These days spirits very low. People don't know one another after the reorganization, also dead tired, also have not had a letter from mother. Even more worried about how to stay alive – was very depressed not to be given the leftover food. Ridiculous. Control it, control it! Keep on like this and will become mean and despicable. Need to calm myself, be generous with people.

Don't be anxious about getting or losing.

Wang Sanyu very good person, has the air of an intellectual.

Picking up cigarette butts every day has become the main meaning in my life. Finding a butt is like finding a treasure.

Afternoon rained, stopped work after three o'clock. Cut stalks while drenched in cold rain, hard to describe how bad it was. Loaned clothes to two people on return to Number. Don't have many clothes but don't mind lending them as clothes are external to the body.

Rice is growing poorly this year, prospects don't look good. Probably won't have rice for a while – every meal now we get wheat chaff instead.

Middle of the night. Troop Leader Yue and Chen Lin suddenly came to each Number to examine clothes. Are preparing to issue cotton-padded clothing for winter. I wasn't greedy, only asked for some cotton padding and two feet of cloth to patch my old clothes. Troop Leader Yue truly is a cadre who lives up to his responsibilities.

25 September

Canal Two harvested rice. Zhao Ying always criticizing Group Seventeen as though we don't work at all. Wang Sanyu very worried after being criticized. He started sobbing in the field when Zhao Ying confronted him. I felt very sorry for him.

26 September

Rain every day, went to Canal Two to bind stalks. Worked all day in the rain, ate lunch in the rain. Truly can hardly get anything done. Stopped work at four o'clock. Again held meeting when we got back; I said that Yu Guozhen and Tan were not performing too well.

27 September

Rain. Went to Canal Two to bind rice stalks. While eating lunch discovered Tan had committed the crime of smearing mud on the rice stalks. Troop Leader Yue held an impromptu criticism-and-struggle session in the field. Supply of food getting tighter, relations among us all getting worse. Little Ding used to be pretty friendly with me; now a pinch of tobacco is out of the question.

28 September

Rain. Early morning did not go out to work – studied as we made hemp ropes. Slept poorly all night. Liu had diarrhoea, crawled over me many times going in and out. At ten o'clock suddenly called to go out to work. Heavy downpour when halfway there, troops called back and returned to barracks. On the way talked about literature with Wang Sanyu, actually felt happy. Wang Gutan talked to me, said he had lost confidence – I tried to comfort him. Afternoon again went out to work, to Canal Three to harvest rice; worked all the way to eight o'clock. By incredible chance got a double helping of dinner.

29 September

Rain. Got out on the road and then turned back. While studying, Troop Leader Yue told me to go to Canal Nine and tell the men working there to knock off work. Ran into Troop Leader Wang who said angrily, 'Stop work? I know!' On return wrote Mama a letter, asking her to write an inquiry to the leaders of labour reform, also to send me some winter clothing. Afternoon they suddenly assigned six new arrivals to our group, all very strange men. Vicious and nasty looking when eating, had to borrow bowls from people, had none of their own. Don't know what kind of case this is.

30 September

Work today relatively easy. Went to Canal Thirteen to harvest soybeans and Canal Sixteen to harvest sunflower heads. Shu Gang discovered Qu eating seeds. The two had a big fight, wouldn't work at all.

1 October

Today is National Day. Morning cut rice stalks, afternoon bound them. Chen Yuzhong began to play dead dog, had diarrhoea, lay on the bank and wouldn't work. Yet he has enough strength left to eat people's leftovers.

New arrivals say that people who don't work hard on the Outside are being sent in to be labour reformed; also said attacks on the Party by bad elements in the villages very intense. One production brigade lost ten of their eleven oxen.

Ate a bun at lunch, which counted as my celebration for National Day. Evening studied and again struggled against Tan. I asked to be allowed to go to the infirmary for checkup. Chen Yuzhong was also waiting in line at the infirmary; said he'd rather be in a regular official labour camp than this kind.

*T*he diary's daily entries indicate pretty well what China was like in the early 1960s, how three hundred and sixty-five days of the year were passed in labour, exhaustion, hunger, eating greens, stealing, fighting, punishment, and study meetings. I do not want or have the ability to present an entire period of history here. This little rivulet I bring the reader does not have brilliant sunshine playing on it, the cavorting of little shrimp, the sweet languor of water weeds. Instead, it is like a dirty ditch, discoloured by the discharge of tanneries and chemical refineries, polluted by the seepage of man's activities. I have followed it into salt fields where the grass has stopped growing, wondering where it will lead. What lies ahead? Will this rivulet flow into the broad reaches of the river of history?

No matter how vividly one writes about the past, it is impossible for words on paper to make a surging river flow again. One omission in the entries must none the less be addressed. In the original text of the diary, death is not mentioned. The entries treat convicts as though they were birds of immortality – the phenomenon of death did not seem to touch the camp.

Back then I did not record it, because I did not dare record it. Now I do.

Leftovers

Reading the diary, it seems that there was more than just one portion being left by just one person. Yes, it was true that when the entire country was suffering from famine convicts would indeed leave in their bowls some of their meagre rations, rations that were measured out in amounts no bigger than the amount of sand in your eyes in the morning.

Had these men eaten too much already, or had their families perhaps sent them things to eat? Not at all.

In those days, as we ate and stared flinty-eyed at the others to see who might have leftover food, we still envied those who could afford to leave it. We thought what a wonderful feeling that must be. Certainly only someone who felt full could leave food uneaten, and to feel full was something miraculous. As we dreamed of this amazing state we were just sorry that everyone was not leaving leftovers so that we could have them all to ourselves.

The fact that I specifically mention leftovers several times in the diary shows the importance I placed on this subject. Nobody bothered to ask why a man couldn't finish such a tiny bit of food. Gradually we came to realize that leaving a meal unfinished was not a pleasure but a terrible omen. Those who could leave food behind had felt the kiss of death.

I watched as various people began to leave food in their bowls. Then those who had been the objects of our envy began to die, one by one. At the time, I remembered only the food they left behind, not the dying.

I think I was the first to notice this peculiar phenomenon; other convicts were still oblivious. Since I was embarrassed to be gluttonously eyeing other people's bowls, my focus on the possibility of leftovers from certain people developed into a clinical examination of their condition.

Han Dianming was an example. It was hard to detect any abnormal symptoms. He could still go to work as

107

usual and his 'labour' was not inferior to others'. But when it was time to eat he was not terribly interested. He dawdled toward the food wagon, leisurely pulled out his bowl, as though he was so enthusiastic about labour reform that he had reached a stage of doing without food and sleep. In less than half a month, a death mask appeared, an increase in eye mucous, a darkening of the skin. After that, a man would either get thinner or begin to bloat. While he was eating, his eyebrows would pinch together, as though he detested eating, even though a thin line of saliva would often flow out from the man's bottom lip. (This would not diminish other people's enthusiasm for getting hold of food directly underneath the drip.) By that time the man would look like a puffed-up brown toad.

In a few more days, the convict would die right there in the field. Most of them died in the day, at work. A man would suddenly collapse. The Troop Leader would yell to the Group Leader to send two convicts who still had some strength in them to carry him back to camp.

'Shock again! Carry him to the infirmary. Let the doctor take a look at him, give him a shot!'

There began to be a daily increase in the number of men who fell over while working and were then unable to get up. Carrying each one back to camp became too much work. The food wagon took on a new responsibility after it had finished distributing food. It would park by the side of the field, waiting for convicts with 'shock', and its daily harvest was considerable. There seemed a derisive symbolism in having the cart that brought life-sustaining food on the way in escort the dead out on the way home.

The first time I heard the word 'shock', a Chinese

transliteration of a Western medical term, it came from the mouth of a Troop Leader who was completely illiterate. What was 'shock'? Later, Zhou told me it could also be called *petit mort*: he said it was the reaction of the body to a disruption in the absorption of oxygen. Some people in a state of shock would actually recover once the doctor administered a shot of grape sugar. But most people went quickly from petit mort into real death, and then were seen no more.

People who succumbed on the workfield and then truly died were not aware of any specific illness before dying. They could not have said which part of them hurt or which part was ailing. To this day I am not at all clear about the medical facts behind this phenomenon. Other than the death mask, there was little indication that a person might suddenly fall over and die. I remember that at the time I became hypersensitive to my own condition: the god of death appeared to like this undetectable manner of making sudden attacks.

I worried that I too would not be able to finish my meal, so that not feeling full after a meal became a cardinal sign of good health. Every day the feeling assured me that for the time being I was not going to die. This made me feel even more hungry. The need for food was not a localized, tangible, limited thing, but had become a supraphysical, comprehensive, spiritual quest. It was a kind of infinite need that transcended a real need. The feeling of hunger was particularly acute when chewing on a millet bun or pouring thin gruel down the throat.

Every group witnessed this phenomenon of leftover food. Each had two or three men who frequently left food in their bowls and who soon became stars among the convicts. They would be surrounded by men who fawned on them more energetically than they ever fawned on a Troop Leader.

I still remember the Qu mentioned in the diary on 20 September. He was a Cantonese, short, with big eyes, a graduate of Zhongshan University who had been teaching physics at a middle school in Gansu Province. He was a rightist, but his real downfall came from having relatives overseas. In 1958, at the start of the Great Leap Forward, he 'released information on the situation regarding the country's internal supply of material goods'. The evidence was in a letter written to his relatives. He probably meant nothing more than food supply, not military secrets – and so they sentenced him to labour reform instead of executing him. He once told me that he had only wanted to have his relatives send him a package of food. He had had no other intention. He still could not figure out how the school authorities came to know the contents of the letter. 'Very strange!' he said. 'The letter hadn't even been mailed off and I found myself here!'

Why did I criticize him in the diary for 'putting a lot into convincing [Han], saying inappropriate things like he would get him medicine, calories, etc.'? Everyone put a lot of work into befriending convicts who had leftovers, including me. Why was that inappropriate?

I remember the reason well. In his petition to Han he would say that from now on Han should give all his leftover food to him and not give any to anyone else; that, since Han could not finish his food, Qu would get him medicine to bolster him. He even worked out for Han how many calories were needed by a man per day. He said that he would have his overseas relatives send medicine to China for him. That is to say, Qu planned to use as collateral on a loan the medical supplements that his overseas relatives would certainly never send him.

He had not severed ties with these overseas relatives in his thinking and was even using his crime to benefit himself in the camp. That was what I found so galling.

In fact, I was somewhat ashamed not to have thought of this tricky way of begging for food myself – but I had no overseas relatives of whom I could make use. Even less did I have never-to-receive possessions that could be mortgaged. My only recourse was to say earnestly to Han that I was extremely hungry – if you cannot finish may I please have some of yours?

On 22 September, Han and I were on duty together. We carried a bucket slung from the same pole and I even made sure the rope holding the bucket hung closer to my end so I would carry more weight. But at every meal he still gave his leftovers to Qu – the future illusory 'supplements' had their effect. A few days later, on National Day, 1 October, Han Dianming was conveniently carried back in the horse wagon that brought out our food. He had not waited for Qu's relatives to send medicine before disappearing from this world for ever.

Each group's rules and regulations differed slightly on the subject of the distribution of food. In order to avoid having the healthier convicts start fights over anyone's leftovers, causing dissension within a group, most of the groups began to require that all leftovers be consolidated and then centrally divvied up. In some groups it was distributed to the convicts who behaved the best, in others it was given in turn to all convicts so that no matter how well or poorly you worked you would get a share.

Wang Sanyu

Most Group Leaders and group members were all the same – they only wished that more and more people would leave leftovers. They were unconcerned about the curious detail as to why people couldn't finish their food. Our Group Leader, Wang Sanyu, was different. He never even noticed who left behind food or who ate it. He himself never asked for leftovers from anyone. On the day that the groups were reorganized, he led us in drafting a new Small Group Guarantee which had among its items the statement 'oppose vulgar interests, oppose talking about nothing but eating and drinking'.

Other than eating and drinking, what else was there to talk about? Unfortunately that Guarantee, together with the work quotas, no longer exists. It would have been an excellent example for intellectuals who idolize literature that talks about nothing. The purity with which it refused to stoop to reality led to our group's loss of control over the disposal of leftovers. For example, it ended transactions like that between Qu and Han, deals that could still be carried out as private exchanges.

On National Day, Chen Yuzhong used the pretext of diarrhoea to 'lie on the bank of the field and refuse to work'. But when it came time to eat, he rather publicly clambered up and begged for people's leftovers. 'The more I have the runs, the more I have to eat, and only if I eat can I do any work.' Somebody already sick of food gave him a spoonful. From the fact that I noted this in the diary and from my choice of words, my position on this can be imagined. If our group adopted a method of centralized distribution too, it would be impossible to have these 'dead dogs' suddenly jumping up to beg for food.

Wang Sanyu had a rather democratic style of leadership. He had graduated from the famous Qinghua University and was originally from Hebei but had been working as an engineer in the Railroad Bureau of Lanzhou when he was labelled a rightist for saying something or other. By the time he was assigned to our group he walked with a lurch, his face was ashen, and he looked like an invalid. He was frequently a Sick Number, but if you asked him what ailed him he would say that the infirmary couldn't diagnose it – he just had the sensation that his lower limbs were tingling or numb. From time to time it was as though nothing below the waist belonged to him. Like the first Group Leader convict to teach me, he led the way in all aspects of our work. He was truly a shining example.

From the diary you can see that our Group Seventeen was subjected to criticism almost every day, so that Wang Sanyu, full of our collective spirit, even had a confrontation on 25 September with the newly arrived Big Group Leader Zhao Ying.

Every day, hands behind his back, Zhao Ying would saunter along the bank of the canal looking for all the world like a cadre. In fact, he had just been plucked from the ranks of the convicts and promoted to high-class convict. As a result, his severity exceeded that of any other Troop Leader. He was always fingering a small notebook, and whenever he approached a field where a group was working he would flip it open. In the book were the labour quotas announced by Station Leader Yan on 19 September.

'Hey! Do you all remember? Harvest: each day one mou two fen. Binding: must be two mou or more. Transport: each person is to haul sixty huali and each trip is not to be less than eighty jin. How do you think you're doing, you bums? When it's time to knock off work, think you'll have it done? If you don't, I'm going to keep you working!'

No matter what the circumstances, however much you cut, bound or carried, he would find a way to raise the ante. Our Group Seventeen had lately been assigned to paddy fields that still held undrained water – in the shallowest part the water came over the ankle. At the slightest misstep you would slip and whack your scythe into your own leg. Harvesting rice was like pulling out hairs on your chin – each stalk was one less to harvest but you would have damaged yourself in the process. Imagine cutting one mou two fen of rice a day under these circumstances.

Wang Sanyu said that Yan 'used a chicken feather as a mark of authority' and conferred on him the title of Mr Doctrinaire. (This was the kind of feeble language an intellectual used to curse people.) When Zhao Ying heard it he laughed out loud.

'Good! Good!' he said. 'You're using the quota announced by Station Leader Yan as a "chicken feather". Fine! Fine! This engineer's awfully full of himself. You just wait . . .' he finished ominously.

An arm can't win over a leg in a wrestling match. Zhao Ying was a cocky little fellow. In terms of caricatures he belonged to the type known as handsome young men. It was said he was a 'male-female relations' convict, the sort who had better chances of being chosen for advancement – the labour camp authorities seemed to respect and enjoy these men. There was no way Wang Sanyu was going to win over him. They argued until Wang Sanyu began to cry.

'You're irrational,' he sobbed. 'You don't make sense! I've never seen anyone as irrational as you!' All he could do was repeat this over and over, as though everyone else doing labour reform was more logical than Zhao Ying.

He did not feel aggrieved because he, a dignified engineer, had come so far down in the world as to be working in a labour reform camp. Instead, his view was rather like my own – we felt that we did our best to argue on reasonable grounds. Members of our group, both new arrivals and old, had never seen a Group Leader so protect the reputation of his convicts. I was not the only one to sympathize with him; everybody else hung his head and felt badly.

Not long afterwards, this Group Leader most worthy of respect, this model convict, entered the hospital of the labour reform camp. He died shortly after disappearing inside.

Wang Sanyu was a clear-cut case of a wrongly judged convict. He wouldn't toady to people, lick ass, or run around reporting on others. Honest and upright – it would be hard to find another like him. So why did the authorities insist on singling him out as Group Leader, raising him to the status of a high-class convict? This engineer, graduate of a famous university, was also a high-class intellectual; no matter what work the country might assign him to do, he did it conscientiously. To him, being Group Leader was even more of a responsibility. He was unlike Su Qin who saw through it all right away, and this ultimately cost Wang Sanyu his life.

They say that at the time he died they still had not been able to work out what sickness he had. He came into the labour camp without any explanation for being there, and he died there without any explanation for leaving. Conscientious intellectuals always pay the least attention to the most important details.

Tobacco

Tobacco was second only to food in importance to us.

I was only twelve years old when I began to smoke. Later when I was infected with a taste for writing poetry, the custom of smoking and the process of writing went hand in hand. The more I smoked the more I needed to smoke, so that by the age of eighteen I was an old hand. I would smoke at least two packs a day. By twenty I had never made love to a woman but my infatuation with tobacco surpassed my desire for sex. On coming into the labour reform camp I never once thought of women, and had none to think about, but tobacco often tempted me out of my mind.

In 1958, each group was still able to allocate a little tobacco on a regular basis, distributing it to the convicts who smoked. Naturally, labour reform convicts could only buy the most inferior tobacco, eight fen for one pack. This was a brand produced in Henan called Double Fish. In addition to shredded tobacco, inside the rolled paper were bits of tobacco twigs which made the cigarettes hard to light. Smoking one cigarette cost you half a packet of matches. Matches were also extremely valuable in the camp – they belonged to the category of things that had a limited supply and so were rationed. People were reluctant to use them, so they would gather scraps of fabric from the trash heap to use as cloth wicks. They would light these in the evenings during meetings and let them burn slowly so that whoever wanted to smoke could use one to light up.

The wicks were like smoke-belching poisonous dragons emitting the stench of the garbage heap, filling the entire room with smoke. We hardly knew if the smoke we were breathing in was tobacco or the smoke of the cloth wicks, which added to the intensity of everyone's coughing. Yet from what I could tell nobody ever died of lung disease in the camps. It is obvious that Chinese lungs are different from Western lungs in that they have built up a strong resistance to pollution.

In the beginning, each convict was able to buy one pack of cigarettes per week. Later this went down to one pack every two weeks, then one per month, then several people split one pack, then two or three people shared one cigarette. In the end, tobacco smoke, like mist, had completely vanished from the air.

Things are valued depending on their scarcity, so eventually tobacco came to be a treasure valued next to food. Those strongly addicted even put it in first place. They could always eat greens when their stomachs were empty, but nothing could relieve the addiction when the need for tobacco came upon them. The commodity most actively traded in the free market had to have been tobacco leaves. With famine stalking the entire country and food in short supply, it was not easy for those Outside to collect edible things to trade in the camp, yet in the beginning at least tobacco seemed fairly easy to obtain. As a result free convicts used various means to bring in tobacco leaves as the basis of their underground market activities.

A good half of my clothes went in exchange for tobacco. Once I traded an Australian leather briefcase for ten small bottles of pipe-tobacco. These bottles were one-hundred-millilitre fish-liver-oil pill bottles, which became the unit of measure in trading tobacco. I dare say that many small fortunes were spent on these bottles.

At first, the tobacco in the bottles was pure. The price of each bottle was linked to the value of a steamed millet bun, just as international exchange rates are pegged to the American dollar. The camp exchange was roughly one bottle to one bun. The values of other goods, such as pants, shirt, hat, all the way to underpants, were figured on this basis. Wherever you find people, you will find a market, and all markets follow the rules of value. If anyone had the interest, he could enrich scholarship in this area by writing a micro-economics analysis of a free market in the yard of a Chinese labour reform camp.

The one to one price existed in the early stages, when tobacco was already in somewhat tight supply. By mid-1960, tobacco leaves in the big yard had a price but no market – even if you had things to trade you couldn't get hold of any tobacco. If you managed to find some, what you got was fake and inferior. Many free convicts quickly became profiteers, unscrupulous merchants. They would pack sawdust from the carpenter's shop into the fish-oil bottles. When they traded this off to you for a steamed bun or some clothes and you took the first puff you could be knocked out by 'shock'. As a result, the diary's notations regarding tobacco trading become more scarce over these last few days. Instead it is 'hard to get even a pinch of tobacco', 'picking up cigarette butts every day has become the main meaning of my life – finding a cigarette butt is like finding a treasure'.

Picking up whose cigarette butts? Thrown down by whom? Only the cadres of the labour reform camps threw real tobacco butts on the ground. This one short sentence in the diary indicates that I was acutely observant of Troop Leaders' slightest movements. After he had started us working, the Troop Leader in charge of leading us to work every day would generally sit on the back of the canal and smoke. First he would walk around the territory he was responsible for guarding, then he'd climb up on the bank, occupy a commanding position and gaze arrogantly over his flock of convicts. When he pulled out a cigarette to smoke at such a moment, it must have tasted particularly sweet.

Troop Leaders who came from peasant families did not follow the civilized practice of putting out their cigarette butts. When they had finished smoking they would just flick the butt aside. Fortunately they still smoked the eight-fen-a-pack brand, Double Fish. These butts would quickly go out when they were tossed onto the ground, and this kind of tobacco was worth my going to pick up. Better tobacco would keep burning until it had turned to ashes, so that when I tried to pick it up there would be nothing left.

Don't look down on all these details – they count as scholarship! I've accumulated too much knowledge of this kind in my life, to the point that I often think I am unable to take in anything more.

We had no tobacco, but we had good policies. Under the policy of lowered-rations-to-be-substituted-with-gourds-and-greens, vegetables, wild grasses, even toads could be substituted for grain. Tobacco could be substituted with anything that would ignite – leaves of trees, shrubs, grass. I personally have experimented with poplar leaves, scholar's-tree leaves, *yushu* leaves, *yang-shu* leaves, sunflower leaves, soybean leaves, hot pepper leaves (which actually have a hot flavor in the smoke) and cabbage leaves (similar to the mildest forms of tobacco). I've tried at least half of all the plants grown in the Great North-west, which is perhaps one reason I still love the Great North-west.

In the end I settled on eggplant leaves as the best. The flavour of eggplant leaves is similar to that of tobacco; I smoked them exclusively for over a year. After getting out of the labour reform camp, I went straight to the most authoritative encyclopedia – the tobacco known as Nicotiana nicotinau spp belongs to the eggplant family. If I had not lost my ties to civilization, I could have looked up what to smoke in a book and not had to experiment with my lungs and throat.

Of course the leaves of these plants do not have nicotine in them, and so cannot stimulate like true tobacco. Can one break an addiction by smoking them? No. On the contrary, they make your head so dizzy you don't know which way you're going, and your throat so hoarse you can hardly breathe. But in times of famine even breathing a breath of air into the innards feels good. Air at lest makes an empty stomach feel like a ball, and from the outside it begins to look nicely rounded. But pure air has no flavour. With some smoke in it, even a strange smoke, the air at least has a kind of seasoning. Strictly speaking, I was smoking not for the smoke but for the air.

Clothes

The reader may not understand a paragraph written in the diary on 24 September: 'In the middle of the night, Qu and Chen Lin suddenly came to each Number to investigate clothes, prepared to issue cotton for getting through the winter. I was not greedy – I only asked for some cotton and two feet of cloth to mend my clothes.'

Issuing prison clothes to convicts should have been like issuing uniforms in the army – one set of clothes per person. Was this to say that in a labour reform camp there was some freedom in what you wore? Yes. According to the World Court, convicts' clothes should be the same; only with special permission or for a convict accorded special treatment should there be an exception. In 1958, when I first entered the labour reform camp, whether we needed it or not, each convict was given one set of prison clothes. The style and cut were exactly the same for both labour-education convicts and proper labour-reform convicts. The shirt was collarless, two pockets were sewn into the outer lower hem of the jacket, and the trousers had no pockets whatsoever. The clothes were the same, but the colours were different for the two classes of men. Labour-education convicts wore purplish blue; proper labour-reform convicts wore black.

In addition to clothes, each convict was allocated one pair of cloth shoes At that time things made of plastic were not common. Hemp rope was stitched together to form a crude sole for cloth shoes. Handmade shoes could not have the same uniformity as clothes, so one saw every style and shape in the camp. Once I was even issued a pair of what people in Beijing call Double Gate shoes.

I don't know where the labour reform authorities found the fabric they issued us. It was so thin that it was like the gauze used by doctors. Through its holes, as Buddhists say, one could view the entire world. Of course, from the outside one could also see everything underneath.

Clothes made from this flimsy fabric wouldn't last any time at all in the strenuous work of labour reform. The shoes were especially vulnerable and were broadly given the name 'holiday shoes'. The speed at which clothes deteriorated in the camps greatly exceeded the country's capacity to supply them, and with political movements sweeping so many innocent people into our ranks, the local government was unable to supply the material. Things were in such confusion that the labour reform authorities were caught unprepared.

The buildings were insufficient to hold the new arrivals. Convicts' sleeping space could be reduced so that barracks could hold more people – from fifty centimetres we were squeezed into forty centimetres, then thirty – but even the most clever government in the world couldn't make two convicts share the same pair of trousers. Finally the authorities had no choice but to allow prisoners to wear clothes they had brought with them into the camps.

The system of unified clothing in the camps was imperceptibly done away with after the Great Leap Forward in 1958. Convicts who came in later, except for those from very poor families, had no hope of being issued any clothes. Officials stopped confiscating convicts' personal belongings – clothes, daily necessities, books. No matter how many cases of things you brought in with you, everything without exception was admitted by the labour reform cadres. Bachelors essentially brought all their household belongings. The camps even encouraged convicts' families to send packages to them. An 'open policy' was instituted in the camps as early as the late 1950s.

This policy established the material basis for a thriving free market in the yard of the labour reform camp. It also provided thieves and poor convicts with unlimited opportunities, and made it necessary to close and lock the doors of Numbers after convicts went to work.

When each convict's bunk space was reduced to between thirty and fifty centimetres, however, a case or box would no longer fit. So convicts extended their universes into space on the walls. Above each person's head they jammed in short wooden sticks. Thick and thin, high and low, these irregular sticks made it look as though a forest of craggy pine trees was arrayed on a precipice above our heads.

All our assorted parcels and belongings were suspended from these sticks. Fortunately no earthquake occurred in those years in that earthquake belt of the Great North-west or the convicts would have been squashed by their own wealth.

The men in the various groups had come from many different kinds of work units. Most had originally been intellectuals or cadres and their belongings included a rich assortment of things. One day in the early spring of 1959, I was strolling around at my leisure as a Sick Number in the big yard and was just thinking of going to do a bit of trading when I saw an old KMT General airing his property in the sun in front of his Number.

The items were spread out on the ground, resplendent in their glory: otter-skin belt, lynx-pelt jacket and hat, a snow weasel windcheater, a long mink coat and a golden-haired monkey jacket . . . also a rare and valuable Baluchistan carpet. He sat on a small stool stretching out swollen legs that already exhibited an oozing yellow secretion. This was another sign of imminent death. His listless face formed a bizarre contrast with the wealth of his treasure, making one think that these items had dropped from heaven into this miserable prison yard.

Soon he did indeed die. He had been thrown into the camp as a double offender, a historical counter-revolutionary and a rightist. After his death, when the labour reform convicts and Troop Leaders mentioned him they would never say 'that reactionary General so-and-so', or the 'thus-and-such position' he had held in the people's government after the uprising, rather it was 'the one with the golden-haired monkey coat'.

I think he may have led a life of some distinction, and it may be that the uprising he led saved many people from being killed in one part of China. But in the end he accomplished nothing, and a golden-haired monkey coat was all he left as his mark in the world. He guarded his treasures closely and couldn't bear to trade anything off in the free market for something to eat. After his death I don't know who took possession of the furs, and who knows where the golden-haired monkey coat went.

As I mentioned, the country was able to produce a large number of convicts but it could not manufacture a corresponding number of uniforms to go with them. It was as though the head of a paternal government had given birth to a passel of children but then was unable to care for them in the most rudimentary way. What to do? We convicts, we pitiful sons and daughters, including those who were said to be anti-party and anti-socialist rightists, were extremely forgiving of the difficulties of our socialist father. Like filial sons, we voluntarily offered up our own belongings and made our own clothes in order to carry on with labour reform.

With all of us dressed differently, one might have thought it would be hard to distinguish between convicts and regular citizens. There were other ways of telling. On the road to and from work and in the fields you could see a multitude of colours and strange costumes. Those in the most wildly patched and variegated garb were convicts.

The appalling thing was not that convicts decked themselves out in outrageous costumes – how could they find any leisure time to worry about fashion? Rather it was that they no longer cared about their appearance at all. They stopped thinking of themselves as fully human, and simply accommodated themselves to the needs of survival, as though they were primates that had not yet developed any aesthetic awareness. Slinging a fur around yourself was not for the looks of it but purely to keep out the cold. If you can imagine one of Peking Man's contemporaries from Zhoukoudian* walking into a department store on Wangfujing Street today, you will have a rough idea of how convicts dressed themselves.

Likening our peculiar clothing to that of beggars would be a mistake, though, since some convicts were still wearing very expensive Western finery. To be pre-

---

* The place south-west of Beijing where Peking Man's remains were found.

cise, they still wore fine silk ties, but they knotted them around their waists to hold their trousers up. If clothes got holes in them, you took a bit of fabric for a patch from wherever you could find it, so that the result was like a Hawaiian shirt. A shirt might be worn outside rather than inside a cotton-padded jacket – if one had no time or was too tired to mend the jacket. Socks were used as gloves; it was usual to see shoes that didn't match. The most common patch for the seat of the trousers was a round-shaped cloth hat. We convicts appeared to be opposed to all convention and restraint – we were the epitome of an extremely modern style.

I must mention the hat I designed. This creation later kept many people from getting frost-bite, so in a sense I will have made some small contribution to this world. With weather particularly cold in the winter of 1959, the camp was having trouble supplying any winter clothes, and the authorities were naturally not going to pass out any nice warm hats. Going against the wind was brutal, the cold pierced our bones; by the time we got to where we were to work for the day our faces would be splitting. Ears would swell to the size of palms in one morning. The cold seemed to find a way to invade any tiny region of warmth, so that snotty, crying convicts would use whatever fabric they could find to wrap around their heads. We would have carried our bedding with us into the fields if we didn't have to do hard labour.

My head was so frozen one morning it had turned to wood, but a piercing wind none the less stimulated it to have an idea. In the evening, during study time, I cut off the leg of a pair of cotton-padded trousers which happened to have a hole at the knee. Other than that, the leg was intact and I used a needle and thread to sew together one end. This formed the top of my hat. Then I sewed shut the lining and outer fabric where I had cut it from the trousers and where the inside cotton padding was exposed. This assured that the stuffing wouldn't fall out.

On the bottom corners I attached two tie-strings and so had an extremely durable, stout, cotton-padded wind-resistant helmet. I wrapped a handkerchief around my face as we went out in the morning and then placed this accomplishment on my head. All that showed through were my eyes. The wintry cold was not going to get me!

The rest of the body stays warm if the head can stay warm. Like a Parisian fashion, this cotton-padded creation soon swept through the labour camp and was on the heads of all the convicts. Think of it for a moment – wearing a pair of trousers on your head. Perhaps the hippie style in the West started in China in the early 1960s.

Once the lowered-rations-to-be-substituted-with-gourds-and-greens policy began, I understood why we convicts were forbidden to have interior pockets in our clothes. Exterior pockets were allowed but no hidden inside pockets. The reason was to prevent convicts from putting forbidden objects or things inside. But convicts are a cunning lot. In order to bring home cabbage, carrots and sweet potatoes from the fields to cook in the big yard, convicts would sew innumerable secret pockets into the prison clothes or their own personal clothing, using cotton fabric or heavy wool.

From the looks of them, Troop Leaders might have thought their convicts were plump and robust. Back home in their Numbers, though, like magicians, convicts would flash open their clothes and the raw materials for eating greens would cascade to the ground. The fat man would miraculously become thin. Those with a natural talent for this act could bring home ten to twenty jin of food at a time.

Years later I was strolling down a street in New York when a man approached and suddenly flung open his coat. Lining this coat were the goods he wanted to peddle. The number of his inside pockets and the profuse variety of objects could be considered a 'modernization' of the fashion begun in China. I had to smile – there is a sameness to mankind wherever you go in the world.

Various clues have been dropped in this section about the conditions in the camps at that time. 'No rice. Ate millet gruel for every meal.' 'Harvested rice stalks in the drenching rain, hard to describe how bad it was.' Every day, 'stopped work very late'. When those near death had leftover food, 'they asked who wanted it and were immediately surrounded by three or four people'. 'Supply of food more and more tight'; some people 'would rather go to an official labour reform camp'. I personally also 'began to feel my heart beat at the slightest exertion', 'was dizzy by mid-day', and so on.

The Double Counter Movement that was rolled into action in 1960 brought large numbers of fresh fodder into the camps. In order to have the older convicts train the new arrivals in the camp rules, and also to have new arrivals motivate the rest of us to work harder, the camp bosses mixed together new and old. Initially this policy was quite effective.

The new convicts came in feeling liberated. The rectification they had endured wherever they worked on the Outside had often been harder to take than labour reform. They were forced to answer interrogations at the hands of zealots every day. People watched them constantly, accompanying them even when they went to the bathroom. Naturally they were not allowed to return to their homes in the evenings. In this new 'free' realm of a labour reform camp they put their backs into labour and reform.

As I wrote in the diary, they 'didn't work too badly'. Yet several days later I also lamented, 'Putting us older ones and the new arrivals together is going to do us in.' Yes, for a short period of time work efficiency in the camp went up. Then people began not finishing their food and the number of those with leftovers began to increase daily. As predicated, the old convicts began to collapse.

It was then that the great numbers of deaths began. They started in September of 1960. This diary stands as evidence.

Earlier incidents of death among convicts noted in this diary could be characterized as the odd, individual death. Although from time to time these occurred by twos or threes, death had still not reached the level of wholesale production. After September 1960, dead men were like goods in an assembly line. They were carried out of the camp's big yard in an endless stream.

4 October

Utterly tired out. Went to Canal Three to harvest rice. Worked through to three p.m. before coming back to the big yard to eat. Ate, then went out to work again. Back numb, legs hurt, head dizzy, eyes seeing stars. Wanted to ask Group Leader for a rest, but to keep face decided not to. Tan Weimin played dead dog after eating and refused to go out, so was hauled before the Troop Leader and told that in the evening he would get half his normal food.

Group Seventeen again rebuked, this time for harvesting rice that wasn't yet ripe. This was discovered by Troop Leader Yue. Wang Sanyu couldn't wiggle out of it when the investigation traced back who was responsible. A new arrival, Sun, had said that paddy rice could be harvested if it was 80 per cent ripe. Actually Qu had gone alone and said it could be harvested, but Wang Sanyu didn't reveal this.

Troop Leaders were given our names; everyone scared, not sure how we would be punished.

14 October

Work these days very tough, harvesting, binding and carrying, slipping in the mud. Really no time to write in the diary. Still no letter from Mama. From the 10th, they cut the grain ration again to fifteen jin. The leaders reported that this amount would be maintained for several months, but who's to say? Wang Sanyu sick, went to stay in the infirmary. Leaders treat him quite well. Xiang Xiaozhong now our Group Leader. I've been sick from around the 11th, fever every afternoon. Went to see the doctor last night who gave me one half-day of rest.

15 October

Letter I wrote Mama was mailed out yesterday. Rested one day in the Number. Small Group went out to dig grass – heard there wasn't much, had already been dug up by neighbouring villagers. Had a 'life improvement' today: was able to eat a grass-bun at noon. Those who went to work said at first they didn't get their food at all. The food wagon didn't deliver to Canal One, so Xiang Xiaozhong went to carry it back for them on his shoulder pole. Should have been buns for thirteen people but one missing. Everybody said it was Xiang who ate it. Back in the big yard, Xiang had a fight with the men in the kitchen.

When we were asleep, Troop Leader Zheng suddenly bolted in and woke everyone up, said we had dug too little grass. Su Dingxin dug only five jin, the most anyone dug was twenty jin. Zheng was violently upset, cursed each of us out in turn.

18 October

Sluggish and dizzy these two days, no strength. Went to dig grass but couldn't get much done. Today another sudden reorganization of groups. Reassigned to Group Twenty-five. People exhausted already, with this happening again it's worse. Attending to one thing you lose the other. Lost two pairs of cotton shoes – luckily when Troop Leader Yue found out next day he had me go to the warehouse to get two pairs in compensation.,

Morning played dead dog, didn't go to work. Feverish every day, coughing in the evening, spitting thick phlegm. Don't know if it's tuberculosis or not. At noon tried to declare Chen Dexiu's name to get a Sick Meal – failed and was sworn at. Am already shameless, no ethics at all. Nothing to give me any self-respect. Morale low, reluctant to talk to anyone, situation ever more desperate.

Many things I want to write these past few days, but no energy. As soon as I get back, need to sleep. Got a package today from Mama, so took up the pen to write again. Quota for grain reduced, dramatic increase in Sick Numbers.* Every day there are nine or ten from our group when they read out the names. There are also many sick people who can't get on the list. Out in the fields when we're supposed to work, a lot of us just lie down. Troop Leaders see it but pretend not to notice – they can't do anything.

6 November

Went to be checked at the infirmary yesterday. Dr Chen said I could rest for a half-day, but when they read the list of Sick Numbers my name wasn't on it. Went to the fields and bound a few bundles of rice stalks. By noon couldn't move. Lay down all afternoon and at four I staggered back. Passed the vegetable field and thought of taking some sweet potatoes, but instead got hit on the jaw.

According to new arrivals, what we eat here isn't worse

---

* A person officially allowed to be on a list of recuperating convicts.

than Outside. How are people on the Outside supporting themselves?

8 November

Physical condition deteriorating. By afternoon couldn't continue working. Always hungry. These last few days boiled green leaves and roots to eat. Yesterday managed to get a cabbage – ate it raw but didn't get diarrhoea. Got another slip for a package from Mama. Troop Leader Zheng gave it to me. Zheng said I was the worst example in the entire troop. Said I refuse to be submissive. Those working in the fields are pressed to the limit. They're cursed at even when they can't move. Have just been kicked twice by Troop Leader Zheng – very upset to have myself kicked like a dog.

*A*fter copying out the above text from the diary, it is hard to believe that the words I wrote back then came from the pen of a poet. One begins to doubt that I *was* a poet. If they wanted to sentence me for a crime, any crime would have done – why should they make a fool of me by calling me a poet!

Today, the more I write the more painful it becomes. The anguish is not in having to re-live the past as I write. After all, I was one of the lucky ones. As things were to develop in China, the Chairman of the country* and the Marshals were dragged along the ground like dogs. I was only slapped around a little. A rope, a fist, a kick – none of these broke my bones or ruptured internal organs. Yes, many convicts died, but the deaths were just a prelude to what came later, including the deaths of the Chairman and Marshals. We were an overture, but the main performance was played by men of real ability who had mounted the stage. Convicts who died were no more than extras in the recent history of China.

But I *was* a poet. I had never lacked the ability to spin out sentences that connected with the rhythm of the world. I had never had to force the words, hammer at them or painstakingly polish them. The first ones that came into my mind hit the mark, and in between the words reverberated just the right innuendos. Yet in 1960 I was writing these wooden phrases. As literature, the text of the diary is pitiful.

The canon of the world's literature is proof that a true

* Liu Shaoqi at that time, not Mao Zedong.

133

writer cannot be stripped of his spirit, whether he is in prison or banished to some miserable place. On the contrary, privation has tended to sharpen inspiration. Classics were written when their authors were suffering the most. We know the heights of literature that an idealistic vision can achieve. We know that an exalted spirit is not constrained by the harshness of reality, but soars above it in a self-created landscape.

So why, when I was thrown into a labour reform camp, when I managed to withstand what could hardly be endured, was I deprived of the small amount of literary talent I once enjoyed?

Fear is not a reason, nor any attempt to avoid detection. If that had been the case my writing could have toyed with the censors, could have run circles around them. I could have used codes to write about the terrifying things I witnessed; I could have written characters backwards to create a reflection of what was properly and all too accurately written in my heart. I could have written so exhaustively that it would be unnecessary today to add any explanations – the text could have stood on its own as a record of history. Who's to say? An intentional obscurity, a range of rhythm, a third-party voice mighty have given my work an avant-garde look today.

Instead, I seemed to have lost all intelligence. I lost my powers of discernment, my intuitive feel for things, my humanity. I lost the literary and human qualifications to be a writer. All that remained was the ability to write raw words. I had not become illiterate, but almost. I could write only in the style of an account book, a running ledger. This diary should have had some literary flavour, but it's no better than a primary-school assignment.

No, my anguish is not because I experienced a fairly painful period in life; in fact, seen from today that time reveals remarkable things about the value of human life. Rather, the pain comes from knowing that even before I was immersed in that hardship I had lost a sense of myself. And the loss came not in the labour camps, but before.

When a person not only is aware that he is being controlled, but accepts the ultimate authority of that control, his psychological defence systems crack. These systems are as brittle and fragile as an eggshell. When broken open, the essence of the individual inside flows out entirely. I believe that whatever talents I had in writing probably flowed away the moment that I bowed my head to write my first self-examination.

A person who is still experiencing the world as an individual voluntarily feels the connection between himself and humanity. In expressing his individuality he is also giving expression to an awareness of his vital relationship with society, people, animals, nature. When that sense of selfhood is lost, through acquiescence to an outside authority, the magic and charm of the world and of human life disappear. In my own case, I could no longer be discerning about the world and write about it. Other than my ongoing physical existence, I lost interest in everything. All I could write in the diary were those desiccated, lifeless words.

I believe that the darkness of that period lay not in the fact that it swept away all essential material provisions for survival. More damaging was the way it shattered the self-esteem of so many people. It cut off their ties with the world and squandered their accumulated wisdom. Revising economic policies can bring back the physical necessities of life. It is more difficult to resurrect wisdom.

The further I get in the diary, the more I celebrate my fortune in being inside a labour camp at that period of China's history, and not outside in regular society. From time to time, as I recall the first half of my life, I feel that whether through the kindness of God or good fortune, the most difficult periods I had to go through in life happened in the most ideal places.

Troop Leader Yan announced the quotas very sternly in our 19 September Autumn Harvest Mobilization. Each convict had to promise to complete a minimum of work quotas per day. Although we were to pledge *en masse* that we would fulfil these quotas, they were, in fact, unattainable and the authorities of the camps did not even seem to care. Harvesting machines have not yet been invented that can accomplish rice harvest quotas like that.

In the process known as binding stalks, it was first necessary to cut the stalks and transport them to the side of the field in order to prevent the rice heads from getting wet and muddy. I wrote on the 22nd that we 'passed rice stalks hand to hand from the middle of the field to the banks'. The entire group formed a long line and passed bunches of stalks over to a dry place where they could be bound.

We used rice stalks to bind the rice in bunches. Two bunches of stalks were placed with heads together, then with one twist the two became a length of rice stalk rope. As for back-hauling, the rules said that on every trip one was to carry at least eighty jin. My entire body, skin and bones included, weighed slightly more than eighty jin. It would have been impossible to carry that much every trip. Every person was to carry stalks for a distance of no less than sixty huali. The irregular boundaries of the rice fields were not like a flat straight highway – one could hardly measure the distance of their twists and turns. Some of the convicts did keep on walking and hauling, however, until both man and burden finally toppled over into the canal. A great splash, and you would look around to see the rice floating on top of the water – the body would already have sunk below. A Troop Leader could insist as much as he liked that the man complete his sixty huali, but this man would never climb out on the bank again. He was home for good.

There was no way we could accomplish these quotas. The labour reform authorities saw how weak their errant family members had become, how little fight there was left in us, and they did not, in fact, sentence us to seven or eight more years. They simply closed their eyes to what was happening.

We did not complete our quotas and we were not punished for not completing them. By that time, if convicts suspected of 'sabotaging production' were struggled against at all, they would simply keel over.

Tan Weimin was the young man who had read my poetry and who was eager to make friends with me. On 27 September, when we were harvesting rice, he 'smeared mud on the rice' and this 'crime' was discovered by Troop Leader Yue. Yue erupted like a volcano and held a struggle-and-criticism session there on the spot. The rest of us convicts crawled up on the bank of the paddy field and sat in a row on the muddy ground with Tan Weimin front and centre. Imagine cutting rice in the watery expanse of a paddy field – it was hard to guarantee that every stalk of rice would be unblemished by a spot of mud. The so-called struggle-and-criticism meeting was just an excuse to allow everyone to point at Tan's nose and yell at him for a while.

I was soon amazed by this newly arrived convict, and not because he had read my poetry. He already seemed to have become an old hand at all this on the Outside. He didn't blink an eye as Troop Leader Yue ordered each of us to swear at him. He stood there cleaning his nose with his finger, seeming to be listening but not really listening, neither refuting anything nor accepting what we said. His nostrils were particularly large, and it took a very long time to dig through the accumulation. In fact, he continued to excavate until the struggle session was over. With an exhibition like that it was hard to form an impression of this man as a stinking intellectual, a lover of poetry.

This jolted me into realizing the speed at which the Outside was changing. People were already hardened to the degree that they could endure tough, grinding treatment. Three years earlier, in 1957, people would still tremble when they were criticized with 'stinking curses', they still had a sense of shame. Today, even a sensitive lover of poetry was oblivious, numb to the ridicule of his fellow men.

On 29 September, six very peculiar new arrivals were assigned to our group. I noted that they had a vicious way of eating, but in fact all new arrivals were like this. It was as though they had long been accustomed to the coercive nature of reform. This gradual retrogression created the conditions for the Great Cultural Revolution and it was through the experience of the Cultural Revolution that the Chinese people completed the process of debasing their own human nature.

On 4 October, Group Seventeen was cutting rice in the fields and harvesting 'rice that was not fully ripe'. Although responsibility was traced back to a couple of people, and the names of everyone in the group were written down, in the end nothing really happened. It was settled by being left unsettled – nobody was punished.

In short, the accommodating atmosphere that prevailed in at least one of the camps in China in 1960 was enough to make it possible to think back to those times warmly. In this climate of accommodation, those who saw things clearly, who kept to the fundamentals of survival and paid little attention to others, were able to live in quite a carefree manner. Some people I have written about, Zhou, Tan, Qu, Su Qin, etc., were like this.

Others like Wang Sanyu and me lived in fear and trepidation. Why? What kept us from just going with the flow? I still wonder. For one thing, being able to see things clearly would help in knowing how to face the world today.

Life was, of course, not always what you would call relaxed. At times a Troop Leader in charge would get agitated and run up and down on the canal bank, rope in hand. From the middle of the field we would see one striding in an erratic zigzag path, whipping and cursing as he went along. The inability of convicts to fulfil a quota was similar to a Troop Leader's inability to complete his own responsibilities. We convicts were all a breed of dead dogs: we did not consider the recording of work our own affair, and if you were going to sentence us to seven or eight years of hard labour nobody in the fields would make any effort to work at all. But if Troop Leaders couldn't meet their responsibilities this would affect what they could report up to the Leaders. So for them our performance had serious administrative consequences – wages, grade levels, personal promotions depended on it.

The only way they could deal with us was to make us work longer into the night, and to beat and curse us. During these days in the diary there is frequent reference to 'finished work very late'. As to just how late, without watches nobody could say. The concept of dividing time into hours, minutes and seconds had lost all meaning, not only in the labour camps but throughout China. It was in any event so late that the sky was too dark to see rice to harvest.

Looking at my diary today, I am amazed to see the sentence, 'very upset to be kicked like a dog'. The innocence of my youth! Compared to what happened later, the kicks of that time were like caresses. Back then, when a Troop Leader kicked someone the movement retained the elegance of a ballet dancer and usually only involved the toe. I was kicked many times but it didn't hurt much. I am ashamed to compare it with what happened to those who died later. I learned in the camps that the foot can be used for many different functions, but I never tasted the experience of being kicked with the heel of a boot – as the Marshals and Ministers later did. Being kicked hurt mainly because my body had little flesh on it – it was just bones – but this was something that could not be blamed on the Troop Leaders. Had I been a little more plump, I probably would not even have bothered to write in the diary about being kicked.

The connecting of mouth and fist did not mean a straight-out beating; it was more in the category of pushing and haranguing. It may have looked violent but the actual force that was transmitted wasn't very great. My face was never swollen from a beating. Writing this now, I can't expect sympathy from readers who have experienced much more cruel behaviour.

Chinese intellectuals have traditionally been beaten by others; floggings with a staff at court started back in the Tang dynasty. High officials were not exempt – even passing the exam to be a *jin-shi*,* entering the cultural heights of the Hanlin Academy, was no guarantee of safety. In the early years of this century, beating seemed to have been abolished after the Xinhai Revolution.** Then it was reinstated with even greater intensity in the 1950s. By the 1960s the practice was extended to regular citizens. As an example of China's accomplishments, the application of certain types of punishment seems to have been most successful – certainly more successful, and more widespread, than the eradication of illiteracy.

One of the characteristics of a revolution is to allow the uneducated to beat up those with an education. Therefore I do not take it as a great tribute to myself to have been beaten, but I also do not regard it as any kind of shame. I just happened to arrive in a period when it

* The first level of official degree-holder, on successful completion of the imperial examinations.
** 1911.

was again fashionable to beat up intellectuals, and I was one of the earlier ones to get hit. I felt upset at the time, but that's about it.

Getting hit was also, of course, caused by my own obstinacy. Nobody was forcing me to steal cabbage or sweet potatoes, or to claim to be someone else in order to get a double helping of food.

I should explain this term 'double helping'. It occurs several times in the diary, so was clearly a major event. Other than packages from my mother, all I thought about day and night was the possibility of this double helping. We convicts in the labour reform camps had a strange sort of mental quirk. Even if the food provided by the big kitchen was just grass soup, or even millet buns that stopped you from having a shit, food from the kitchen was still considered a proper meal. If your family sent packages of far better things to eat, food that was full of nourishment, those packages were nevertheless considered a 'snack'. They weren't real food. And if at every meal you didn't have any real food but only snacks, you wouldn't feel that you had truly eaten.

I watched a lot of convicts whose families were relatively well off eat the things sent to them before every meal to 'pad the lining' of their stomachs. After their stomachs were properly padded, they would, with all due solemnity, pour the already cold millet gruel down their throats as though it was far more delicious than whatever their families had sent them. But mouthful by mouthful, everything in those packages had been carefully and minutely saved out of the family's own grain rations. One can imagine how unbearably delicious each mouthful was.

I'll never forget the snacks of a convict from the north-west whose family regularly sent him 'beef noodles'. These noodles made me drool with desire. The food probably came from a tradition passed down from his horse-riding ancestors – it was a kind of dried protein that remained edible and nourishing for a very long time. First you took beef and cut it in thin strips and dried it. Then you threw it in a stone pestle and ground it until it was powder – you can see how well dried the beef had to be first. Then you sprinkled some flour over it and mixed the two together. Eating this mixture was supremely convenient – you poured on boiling water and that was that. Indeed, you could also eat it as it was without any boiling water. With one spoonful of this inside you, you wouldn't feel hungry all day. Plus it had plenty of what Qu called calories – indeed it could be used to feed today's astronauts.

But convicts who ate such good things as this would still not feel fed by it. They would have to have their proper meal, grass soup, millet gruel, etc., before feeling satisfied. Was this because the proper meal had been earned through their own hard labour and so was specially valued? I am still puzzled by this mind-set. I set it down here for psychologists to use as source material in their research.

Since the food produced by the big kitchen was so precious, it was the greatest good fortune to be able to get a double portion of that grass soup or millet bun. Those the leaders regarded as high-class convicts were usually the ones who got that special treatment. Naturally the Troop Leader would not just tell a Group Leader that he was entitled to two helpings – you had to rely on developing your own good relations with the cook. Authorities would occasionally ask convicts their opinion of the food – but the opinions had to be reported up through the Group Leaders, so the cooks naturally treated the Group Leaders with respect.

Under favourable circumstances, when no one was standing nearby, a cook would add a bit to a Group Leader's helping, top it up. Generally those Group Leaders with the best relations with the cooks would be the last to get their food. A leader would go to the window and say a few words as though saying a prayer, and then leave the window with perhaps twice his regular helping. When Zhou exposed Chen Lin for getting a double helping, this was the way Chen Lin got it. As accountant, I would often be in line for food just after the Group Leader, and I would overhear the whispered incantations. They were more powerful than the 'Open Sesame!' of Ali Baba's forty thieves.

There were also Group Leaders who were not aware of this system of double helpings or who did not know how to handle it. Wang Sanyu belonged to the category that strictly abided by the rules. He never used the title of high-class convict to his own benefit. Every time I got food just after he did, I felt sorry for him – sometimes it was so bad I wanted to lean over and teach him a few words.

28 September was a cloudy day. Our group harvested rice until eight in the evening. (The Troop Leader said it was eight o'clock when we stopped working although it may have been ten o'clock; when we started work he might say it was three o'clock when at the most it was two.) Heading back to the big yard, the sky and earth were black as lacquer: the kitchen window alone glowed from the light of a horse lantern. That cheerful yellow glow was like a beacon – it was the only ray of

light in our world, shining all the way into our hearts and almost warming our stomachs. Seeing it, I felt that I understood the profound implications of words we had parroted and misused for so many years: glorious, resplendent, shining.

I had just returned from getting my food with the Small Group when I saw Wang Sanyu collapsed from exhaustion, lying face down on his bunk, immobile. I asked if he wanted to eat – he waved his hand very slightly and told me to get it for him. After I had eaten my own pasty brown millet gruel and was going to get Wang Sanyu's, I thought I would also ask the cook for some boiling water to rinse my bowl. That could, after all, be thought of as gruel as well, just thinner. So I took both my bowl and Wang Sanyu's bowl to the kitchen.

Nobody was lined up in front of the window by then – most of the convicts in the Numbers had already gone to sleep and I could hear the clanging of the cooks inside washing dishes. At the window, at our one shining spot in the universe, I first passed Wang Sanyu's bowl over, saying, 'Group Seventeen, belongs to Group Leader Wang Sanyu.' The cook plunked a ladle of millet gruel in the bowl. Next I passed in my own bowl and the cook barked out, 'Whose!' Because he could only see within the circle of light – outside the light all was blackness – because I had held back my anxious desire for second helpings for so long, because of my alertness and also my luck, I instantly swallowed back my request for hot water.

'Huh?' I said, as though it was the most natural and rightful thing in the world to ask for this helping of food, as if it was unnecessary even to ask. And I followed that with an exclamation that was somewhere between 'motherfucker' and 'what's it to you.'

The cook did not ask twice. As though hypnotized, he plunked another ladle of soup in my bowl.

So I wrote joyfully in the diary, 'By chance got a second helping of food!'

I slurped up the whole of this second helping on the way back to the Number, where I gave Wang Sanyu his own helping.

It should be realized that all incantations are chanted in meaningless syllables. Like the chants of esoteric Buddhism, one intones a few notes over and over to make the connection between yourself and the deity . . . or with the person in power, to indicate your familiarity with him.

Since getting a double helping was underground activity, requiring fairly abstruse scholarship, most convicts like Su Qin were oblivious to what was going on. Wang Sanyu mistakenly thought that 'the Group Leader doesn't even get one additional mouthful of food', and so he resigned. As a result he forfeited an extremely hard-to-obtain opportunity. Indeed, he turned down his one chance to survive.

After Wang Sanyu want into the infirmary, someone named Xiang Xiaozhong became our Group Leader (see 14 October in the diary). This Mr Xiang thought it sufficient merely to be Group Leader in order to get a double helping. The next day at work he helped himself to a second wild-grass bun. Members of our group had one less as a result, and they made such sharp comments to him that he couldn't squirm out of it. After work he went to the kitchen and had a big fight with the cook. He was wrong about this, too. He should have arranged it all with the cook beforehand. These two examples show that some convicts simply did not know how to get second helpings.

Nobody sent me things to eat from the Outside. The packages from my mother never included food. I often stole cabbages and potatoes, 'picked some roots and leaves and boiled them', but those things were only snacks. I had been looking forward to a double helping of real food for a long time. Although as accountant I approached the status of a high-class convict, I was not one. I could understand more than a normal convict did about how special privileges were granted, but still not actually enjoy them. Knowing the mysteries but not having the status to take advantage of them put me in an extremely painful position. Right now in China the concept of a frontiersman, a pioneer, seems terribly romantic, someone set in the midst of unbearable hardship. That's about where I was.

October 18: 'Morning played dead dog and did not go to work. Feverish every day, coughing in the evenings, spitting thick phlegm.' From September onward I began to feel the steady approach of death. People nowadays often say that vitality comes from activity, from exercise. That is greatly mistaken. Life is preserved in inactivity, in not moving. Back then, if I made the slightest movement, even to lift my arm, I would feel that I had forfeited a second of my life. Life is akin to smoke or mist in the bones – you wave your hand and some of it disappears. Only by remaining still every second, with arms crossed and head hanging down like a ball toward your knees can you continue to hug life into your body.

A fever every day could burn up a lot of calories. Even thinking about it was terrifying. As for spitting thick yellow phlegm, how in the world was that yellow phlegm created? From what material inside the body? Could it be the brownish millet gruel? But there wasn't as much gruel going in as there was phlegm coming out – spitting a mouthful of phlegm was like spitting out a mouthful of my life.

I began to try to analyse what was so bad about death anyway. It was hard to say, but a fear of death seems to be in the subconscious of all animals. If, at that time, some god had told me that I would be able to enjoy feeling full after dying, I would have summoned my remaining strength and smashed my head against a wall. But gods are least willing to open their mouths when we most need their instruction. All I could do was follow my own groping rules of self-preservation, such as not moving, in order to try to stay alive.

On 18 October a convict named Chen Dexiu died, which alarmed me so much that I was even less willing to move. Chen was an old-timer in the camp who had just been transferred to my group, now Twenty-five. I hadn't even had a chance to look him squarely in the eye before they carried him out. He had his head hung low when he walked into the Number carrying a roll of bedding under his arm. When he left it, it was the same bedding that covered him and I still hadn't seen his face.

The name of the newly organized Group Twenty-five's Group Leader is not in the diary but I still have a vague impression of him. To know him for only a few days and yet to have a lifelong impression was due entirely to his respectful attitude towards death. It was clear that he had been a Group Leader in a labour camp for a long time. From that day onward I have always taken someone's silent regard for a corpse as a sign of that person's maturity.

After a moment he said quietly, 'Who died?'

Just assigned to this new group, the rest of us living convicts had not yet had time to get the names straight. Yet here, in the blink of an eye, was a nameless corpse. The Group Leader frowned with concentration and stared at a name list the Troop Leader had given him.

'Right. Name is Chen Dexiu.' Having found a likely name, he sounded a bit relieved, even glad. 'He's the one! Name is Chen . . . De . . . xiu!'

Our group now had this dead person amongst us, but that was no excuse to waste time that could be spent in working. As the Group Leader gave orders for some of us to carry out the body, he ordered the rest of us out to work. 'Out, out, out! What's there to look at anyway!' Leading the way, he marched out the door of the Number, then stood there preaching as the others came through. 'Out you go! Today you'll be digging grass. Easy work! First off, you get to sit down to do it. Secondly, you get to eat some grass!'

Like a howling child, he added, 'All out! You'll be in trouble if you don't go out today!' This was because he had noticed me still lying on the bunk, reluctant to move. He hesitated, probably because, after all, I was the accountant, then slapped his hands together. 'All right, you stay home and watch over things.'

And so I was left behind to be guard. The dead man was carried out on a wooden plank, suspended from carrying poles. The four convicts carrying it were barely alive themselves. The ropes swung back and forth, letting the plank bang into the door of the Number. The dead man in his bedding rolled a little.

After they had banged out of the door, the Number and yard seemed abnormally quiet. In the stillness the Group Leader's words echoed in my brain. 'Chen . . . De . . . xiu . . . Chen . . . De . . . xiu . . .'

The three words had come together to form a man's name. Once the man had died, the name itself seemed dismembered. It no longer had any significance beyond being three single, dispersed, words. I could see myself being carried out in the same way, bones banging against the door of the Number, making it rattle. The big yard of the labour reform camp and the entire world disappeared before my eyes as I, too, seemed to enter the great void.

But at noon the cook stuck his head out the kitchen window and shouted towards the empty yard that food was ready. All convicts who had stayed home that day were to come and get it. The timbre in his voice was rich and deep, like the self-satisfaction of someone who has recently eaten well. The sound reverberated for a while and seemed to be positively infused with the smell of a steamed bun. I was gripped with envy. After my experience in getting a second helping on 28 September, I had a sudden inspiration.

'The dead have not really died,' I told myself. 'They are standing nearby to help us!' And so I picked up two bowls and marched resolutely to the kitchen window.

I passed in the first rice bowl. The cook didn't even glance at me before slopping in a ladle of millet gruel. I then stiffened my backbone and handed in the other rice bowl.

This time the cook grabbed the bowl and turned to stare at me, eyes burning as he demanded, 'Whose is this?'

I knew instantly that things did not look good. I was all too visible this time, in the daylight, and my situation was also pretty clear. Not only could he see me with absolute clarity, he watched as an unaccustomed red flush came over my pallid face. Still, I had set my course of action and I was not going to retreat. I had also glimpsed the bucket full of millet gruel behind him, giving off a cloud of hot, fragrant steam. It was enough to make a person throw caution to the wind, so I nonchalantly replied,

'For Chen Dexiu.'

Two thick fingers plucked a gruel-smeared list from the counter beside the bucket. The man glanced at it up and down, then smashed it against my face as he flared with anger. 'You motherfucker! Chen Dexiu? Since when was he resurrected? You dogshitters sit there in your Numbers pretending to be sick. Now you pretend a dead man's able to eat this food! Stinking trick! Watch out – you'll be a ghost pretty soon yourself! Wait till you're dead to try to get a second helping! Scram! If you don't move it we'll see what Lao-zi does with you!'

He scooped a bowlful of dirty water with the extra bowl as he spoke and was on the verge of flinging it at me. His movements were supremely quick. Luckily there was a wall between us. He didn't resent me so much that he was going to climb out the window just to come after me. I spun around, used my rear to guard my own precious bowl of millet gruel, and ran.

I hadn't known I could still run so fast.

Back in the Number I held back the tears as I drank my millet gruel. It did not seem as tasty today as it had in the past. I thought about this and thought about how the labour reform camp had become very strict about being on guard against second helpings, to the point that they instantly notified the cook when a person died. The speed of this information flow was probably much faster than the speed at which reports were submitted up to the higher bosses. The cooks were mostly illiterate but by great misfortune I seemed to have run into one who could read. On a paper minutely covered with the names of dead men, he had instantly found the three characters Chen Dexiu. But how could a literate person come out with such crude language!

The new Group Leader had been right. 'You'll be in trouble if you don't go out to work today!' As they say, if you try to steal a chicken you end up losing the rice you use as bait. The bowl I gave the cook had been confiscated too. Lost, and for nothing.

Convicts not only contributed their own clothes as they worked to reform themselves, they also mobilized the reserves of their own existence for the public good. Some people merely brought forth their physical reserves – their idealism and sense of value had long since been stripped away. It had gone in political movements, in criticizing and struggle. By the time a man entered the labour reform camp he was generally already naked in terms of a sense of pride and of a personal character. If he could protect his physical being, this sort of person would survive and indeed live fairly well in the camps. And when he got out of the camps mankind would discover that it had added to itself an individual thoroughly at odds with the rest of humanity. Such a person would often refuse to have anything to do with his own family.

A few were different. These had families who sent them things to eat so that they got more to eat than the average convict, even more than what the family got itself. Since they did the same work as the average convict, they were able to preserve their life force or add to it, and sometimes they were even able to preserve their sense of humanity. Ma Weixiao was such a person.

Then there were those who had considerable reserves but whose characters had been warped by what they heard and saw and lived through in the camps. Their reserves of character turned into 'damaged goods', so that when they got out of the camps they turned into different people. In terms of ideals and beliefs they went to one of two extremes. Either they maintained an attitude of denial or derision toward everything, or they changed whatever their calling had been and took up some kind of religion. Whatever they did, they were fanatical about it – they became zealots.

The saddest were those whose reserves of character were greater than their reserves of physical life force, and who had to consume their physical reserves faster than they lost their character. This kind of convict died.

It can be seen from the text of the diary that I was ashamed every time I did something 'bad'. The warning 'control it, control it' occurs a number of times. Of course, I did not actually give up doing anything bad – when offered the chance I would still steal things to eat, or try to get double helpings, and I learned quite effectively how to pretend to be a dead dog. I would flatly lie down and refuse to work. Still I was relatively clear about my own behaviour. 'I don't have any moral character to speak of now.' 'I'm nothing to be proud of.' This kind of self-chastisement was also a psychological torment. The deeper the character reserves a person brought into the camps from Outside, the more severe the mental pressure.

This conscientious kind of convict was faced with a double adversity. Talent and abilities were gone, but moral beliefs remained. People were like insects who have had their wings cut off and been dropped into a speck of sticky resin. They were restrained by this tiny bit of morality and belief, and found it impossible to fight their way to a carefree existence in their new world. In the end, they shrivelled up, then died in that tiny drop of morality. If they were lucky, someone might find them many years later in a piece of amber.

Nowadays I often think of myself as nothing more than a fly in a piece of amber.

I will never forget the look in Wang Sanyu's eyes just before he left for the infirmary.

The sky was overcast but bright that morning as we crawled out of bed under the shrill demand of the whistle. We hurriedly pulled on our clothes as usual, rolled our bedding, picked up our bowls, and sent a man to check on the status of the big bucket of millet gruel. Those who generally went to the bathroom before breakfast ran out holding their trousers up. Some looked for a belt, some yelled to ask where their shoes had gone. Those convicts with private goods crouched in a corner, their faces to the wall and backs to the others, stretching their necks out as though praying while they swallowed down their 'beef noodles', lining their stomachs before they had their proper meal. Those with phlegm coughed up to heaven like opera singers, trying earnestly to clean their throats before receiving the benediction of millet gruel. Some were already in the process of pleading with those who might leave leftovers, swearing that they could give even better things to eat in return. The straw on the ground was trampled by the comings and goings, swishing like a tornado cutting across a prairie.

The Number was busily and unceasingly in motion . . . the key person, however, our Group Leader, lay still on his bunk. By the time the man sent to the kitchen came back to report that the gruel was reaching an ideal level, at its thickest, people realized they had better urge him to hurry up and lead them out to get it.

He struggled painfully to get up from the bunk. His hands were pressed against the rice straw on the ground, his upper body swayed back and forth, as though some wild beast had caught hold of his legs and he was unable to extricate them from the embrace of the bedding's jaws.

He had never pretended to be sick when he was not really sick. I climbed across several bunks to ask him where he hurt. He didn't say, just shook his head. I felt his forehead – it was wet with a cold sweat, unlike my fever. Writing these words, my hand again feels the sensations of that moment. His skin seemed rough, like a sponge with many holes in it, and my palm almost covered his forehead. His entire head could have been cradled in my hand – I had never realized how small a man's head can become, like the head of a child's doll.

I panicked a little. He had not gone to the infirmary yesterday to get a slip. Would the Troop Leader allow him to rest today? He was not one of those convicts who played dead dog, so if the Troop Leader wouldn't permit him to stay there was no way he was not going to work. And yet, if he went to work he would be throwing away his life. At the same time, I was also worried that if he couldn't climb out of his bedding nobody would lead us out to get our food.

I propped him up in a sitting position. I asked him if he wanted me to stand in for him and get food. This time I had no intention of asking for a double helping because his expression so scared me that I too almost broke out in a cold sweat.

'No need to worry,' he said. 'When you go to work please have a word with Troop Leader Yue for me. Tell him that the lower half of my body won't seem to move.'

Everyone knew that he always walked with crooked legs. So I figured that the old problem with his legs had kicked up again. Although he was clearly in pain his spirits were good and his voice was vigorous. So, as accountant, I led the rest of the men in lining up properly and marching out for our usual attack on the kitchen. On the way I saw Troop Leader Yue looking very grave, hands behind his back as he strode through the big yard. I reported with lowered head that Wang Sanyu was sick.

'He was fine yesterday!' was his retort. 'How can he be sick today?'

In those days all leaders had mastered a method of diagnosis that had begun in the Great Leap Forward: those who had previously been well could never be sick in the future! If Wang was not sick yesterday it was simply impossible for him to be sick today.

On 14 October I wrote in the diary, 'The leaders treat Wang Sanyu pretty well.' In fact, 'leaders' referred only to Troop Leader Yue. After the Great-Leap-Forward-type diagnosis, Yue returned to his normal way of looking at things and asked me what was wrong with him and how bad it was. I said that I wasn't sure but in any event it was serious. His two legs would not move at all, he had cramps and was shaking all over, and he didn't want anything to eat. This last sentence was obligatory as ultimate proof of the gravity of the situation.

When Troop Leader Yue heard this, he poured out on me his anger at the various misdemeanours he had seen in the yard that morning. 'You dogshitters are good for nothing. You say you try to go to work. You say the waist is willing but the legs won't follow. You fall over and say you can't get up. You say this one's sick, that one's sick: who in hell is really sick? It's all a big show put on to trick me!'

I happened to be there at the right moment to serve as an escape valve for his anger. Whether or not he allowed Wang Sanyu a day of rest was beside the point; the main thing was for the rest of us to get some life-saving food in us.

Just as we were slurping down the millet gruel, a doctor carrying a doctor's bag appeared outside the door of the Number. In addition to the bag, he had a face mask over his mouth. I had been in the labour reform camp for two years and other than the regular checkups for 'environmental hygiene' had never yet seen a doctor come into the camp's big yard. They avoided convicts like the plague. Don't even dream of having one come to pay a housecall in a Number! A doctor's appearance at this time could only have been set in motion by Troop Leader Yue.

This doctor was very clever. He noticed immediately who was not eating millet gruel and so knew who his patient was. He didn't even ask – in three strides he had reached Wang Sanyu's bunk, taken out his thermometer and rammed it into Wang Sanyu's mouth. He then pressed his stethoscope to Wang's bony ribs a few times. In the same manner, he didn't ask Wang Sanyu where he hurt or what was wrong. Within a minute he had pulled out the thermometer and stuffed it back in his bag without looking at it. Then he stood up and from within the face mask came the muffled message, 'Get his things together. This one's going to the hospital.'

It should be documented at this point that a man named Qu, mentioned earlier, was not such a bad person. On 14 October, the entire Group Seventeen committed the major crime of harvesting rice that was not yet ripe. It was because of Qu that we did this, but when Wang Sanyu was being yelled at by the Troop Leader he did not say it was Qu's fault. Now, as the doctor spoke into thin air, addressing nobody in particular, Qu immediately put down his bowl and came to help Wang extract his legs from the bedding. He then helped him, with great difficulty, into his trousers.

I licked my bowl clean and also came to help him organize his belongings. Wang Sanyu had only a few ragged clothes, which I stuffed into a pillowcase. This was a brand-new pillowcase he had never used before – hand-embroidered on its snowy whiteness was a pair of mandarin ducks swimming beneath a willow tree. Red alternated with green in the exquisite stitching, which looked incongruous against the filthy wet straw bedding. In addition, Wang had two or three hundred books that he had always spread underneath his body, serving as a kind of mattress.* I pulled these out and stacked them up, large books and small books, but could not find any string with which to tie them. The only thing to do was leave them loose and ask the other convicts to help carry them to the door. Troop Leader Yue had already ordered a couple of free convicts to push over a handcart which was by now waiting outside the Number.

All hands and feet, the men of Group Seventeen helped carry their Troop Leader outside. They placed him flat on the handcart where his thin body lay like a stick. Even with rolled mattress and bedding he occupied only a small area in the middle of the cart, so we stuffed the books around him on either side. Most of the books related to railroad engineering. There were only two works of literature – Ostrovsky's *How Steel is Refined* and Isakevsky's *Selection of Poetry.*

When I tucked these two in beside him, he lightly touched my wrist and smiled as he said, 'Take them with you. You love to read.'

On 28 September I had written in the diary, 'Discussed literature with Wang Sanyu on the road, felt extremely happy.' What we talked about then had been these two books. Their leather covers were made from thick cow's hide, but the pages inside had been turned so often they were ragged. From time to time, either on a rainy day when we didn't go out to work or while he was eating his gruel, I would see Wang reach under the straw on his bunk and pull out one or other of these two books – so

* Chinese books are normally soft-cover and much smaller than books in the West.

159

I knew that in the infirmary he would need them even more.

'You take them,' I put them in the cart with him after all. 'You can read as you're getting well. "An inexhaustible pleasure," ' I quoted.

Then, gently, I added, 'Still remember? "The most precious thing a person has is life. Life is something we get to experience only once. In remembering the past, one shouldn't regret the wasted years, in thinking of the present one shouldn't feel bitter at the pervasive mediocrity. It is enough to be able to say in the end that one's entire life and strength were devoted to the most glorious enterprise on earth: the struggle to liberate all of mankind." '

The two of us exchanged a warm glance as we parted. This oft-quoted and much-loved passage came from the book *How Steel is Refined*. Ostrovsky could never have dreamed that one day it would be quoted by intellectuals in a labour reform camp – a camp in a communist country that had incarcerated as enemies of communism people who, in fact, yearned for a true communist system. He could never have known that his words would be used by political prisoners to encourage each other to persevere, to stay alive, to continue to reform so that they could, once again, take up the task of instituting communism.

Hearing me quote the words 'life is something we get to experience only once', Wang Sanyu looked up towards a sky that was already showing the blue of a new day through the mist. I saw his eyes soften. They showed a fierce love of life, for the world, for people, for work. His spirits seemed to waver momentarily, then gathered strength until in the end his eyes were shining with a light of excitement. He looked as though he was not going to a stinking infirmary, little better than our Number, but would soon be returning to a post where he could put his specialized field of knowledge to use. He was headed out again to build railroads for the country.

Not long after, when the Numbers had been reorganized, we heard that he had passed away in the hospital.

Remembering that scene, and his last look, I always had the impression that he had been buried in a pile of books. The handcart had not yet passed through the gate of the big yard when the books piled on either side of him began to move, then slid over to cover him. From being his bed and his support, they had become his coffin. Because he was a convict, it would not have been appropriate to put a national flag or a party flag over this coffin. But I think it might have been all right to cover him with that exquisitely embroidered mandarin-duck pillowcase.

As I write these notes I appreciate the poverty of language. It may be why other art forms strike a more responsive chord in man's emotions. In 1960, because of what one could call objective conditions, I was limited to writing 'difficult to describe the hardship'. Those objective conditions no longer exist today, but I still cannot adequately express the meaning behind those words. I can't make the reader know the feel of them in his bones. People believe wrongly that language can connect people. In fact, those who have not lived through similar experiences in life do not share the same language.

History has given us innumerable lessons, wise men have given us plenty of warnings, but people continue to court disaster as they go on repeating the same mistakes. I fear that even after writing so much about things I personally experienced, it is probable that this dark period in China's history will happen over again. Even now there are many who not only are unwilling to mention that period but who zealously sing the praises of those who created it. They recall, with great fondness and zest, that 'beautiful' time.

The end of 1960 was probably the worst time in my life. It is hard to imagine it now: we were at peace, there was no war going on. Why was it necessary to put thousands of men in the fields in drenching cold rain and make them stay out there to eat their meagre meals? It was not so very far to go back to the barracks – including eating, the whole lunch would have taken perhaps half an hour.

Agricultural production was originally meant to provide convicts with our basic living requirements. Later, production came to be regarded as a number used to fill a target quota. Still later, production came to be something that was necessary to keep people from being idle. The results of production were measured simply by the fact that men were doing something. One only had to see everyone working, doing unending hard labour, to be able to declare that production was going up.

In fact, the rice that we raised was blighted and useless – many husks were empty. It would have been better to leave the rice stalks in the fields as fertilizer for the soil. But since our Great Leader, born of a peasant's family, could convince himself that one mou of land could produce one hundred and sixty thousand jin of rice, blighted grain had to be included in our figures to make up the numbers.

So we worked night and day, taking no account of driving wind and rain. We were to 'work hard, work bitterly hard'. This was the exhortation promulgated by the Great Leader to his people. On 19 September, when the camp assembled all the convicts for the Autumn Harvest Mobilization meeting, Troop Leader Yan emphasized this slogan over and over again. 'Work Hard, Work Bitterly Hard.'

Mao Zedong was adept at modifying political slogans to meet the times. In 1958, when I had just entered the camp, what we were told was 'Work Hard, Work with Imagination'. This still allowed the intelligence and talents of intellectuals a little bit of room, something for which to aim. There was still just this little bit of respect for science and technology.

By 1960, intelligence and talent were useless. Science and technology were also unnecessary, so that what was left was sheer physical labour. The mentality behind Work Bitterly Hard matched the slogan perfectly. In fact, only intellectuals responded to the different messages in the different slogans. If told to work ingeniously they would think up all kinds of clever ways and means, even inventing a new recipe for steamed buns that were made from rice straw. The more you ate, the faster you died. Told to Work Bitterly Hard, they would throw themselves into it, dredging forth their last reserves of strength; told to do something they would do it, and the more they did it the faster they died.

Criminal convicts learned not to accept this very early

on. An example is Chen Yuzhong, that beggar of left-overs who on 1 October said indignantly that he would rather go to a proper official labour reform camp than this place. He told me that going to hell would be better than staying here. The standard Chinese approach to getting out of a tight spot is as follows: if the situation is not good among people, then see how it works in hell. If the first level of hell is no good, go to the second; if the second stinks, press on to the third. As for heaven? Don't even think about it. Naturally, we, too, have occasionally dreamed of a beautiful future, but it has too often turned into disaster. Experience has therefore trained us to think only in terms of bad things, never to dream for a better future.

Suddenly, at this exhausted and traumatic time, doing labour that was utterly without significance or reward, there appeared an external force that operated on and controlled those who in turn controlled us. This power allowed us to sit at home, out of sight of bosses. We could even lie down and sleep. And so we came to have infinite appreciation for that external force, we came to hope for it every day.

That external force was no more than very hard rain. A drizzle wouldn't do, that would only increase your misery. It had to be buckets of torrential rain.

The heavier the rain, the happier the convicts became. They applauded it and rejoiced in it, but the rain had to fall during the daytime to be of any use. We had a proverb: 'Rain at night, clear in the day, makes a convict so mad his stomach burns.' The proverb is plain and direct, a good example of convict language.

A fondness for hard rain is something I have kept to this day. It has been thirty years since my first experience of a labour reform camp. I now have work that I like, but every time I encounter a rainy day I put down my task, no matter how important, and go to sleep. The sound of rainwater rushing through the gutters of the eaves is the music I love most. That sound can send me into a frame of mind both melancholy and deeply content. It is distant and intimate, raucous and serene. In the swishing sound of rain, I either lie out straight in my bedding or curl up and let every nerve relax, let every cell in my muscles open. With exquisite appreciation, I feel the gladness in my heart and the relaxation of my body. At such times I can hear the various messages of nature passing through the rain. The humidity seeping into the room is a natural element between heaven and earth which gradually surrounds me, melts me, leads me to the state that ancient Daoists once sought. It takes me where the spirit is elevated to a point of not existing, where the open mind is at a pinnacle of awareness. Where, spoken or written, words fail to convey anything but a superficial understanding of what Daoists take as constituting the only element in the universe.

Because of the effect that rain still has on me, I don't in fact believe that people can so easily forget the past.

On 28 September it rained all night then kept on in the morning. The Troop Leader and convicts researched the bubbles stirred up by raindrops that were pummelling the puddles. If the bubbles immediately broke open, that meant the day would clear. If they floated here and there on top of the puddle, then it was certain it would continue to rain. According to this farmers' meteorological lore, it looked as if today it would be raining till nightfall. Convicts were therefore assigned to 'study while you plait together straw ropes'. Production and reform – one was not to miss out on either.

Plaiting ropes was easy and everyone worked away in high spirits. But by ten o'clock the farmer's lore began to fail and the rain diminished. The Troop Leader's copper whistle sounded shrilly through the yard once again. 'Everyone gather right away! Prepare to go out to work!' Making ropes was not considered work.

Like the burst bubbles, everyone's hopes evaporated but the only thing to do was to go out in the rain. Heads hanging low, we stomped along in the mud, weaving back and forth as we headed for the fields. Weary feet sloshed through muddy water; sucking sounds came from all directions. Fortunately the mud of the loess plateau is both finely grained and soft. It doesn't get too slippery and it doesn't stick completely to your feet – otherwise the entire line of men would have slipped and fallen, and never been able to get up again. These were men so feeble that they could scarcely raise their legs, never mind slogging through muddy fields.

As we walked along, the mountains in the west looked as though they were floating in black clouds. Finally the rain came down again. The convicts picked up interest; their mood improved. With hands hugging their shoulders they now stood still, neither moving forward nor daring to run back home. Looking this way and that like chickens stretching out quivering necks in the pounding rain, they silently waited for the Troop Leader's life-saving blow on the whistle.

By this time the whistle was clogged with rain. The Troop Leader tried but couldn't blow a real note, just a little breathy peep as though he and the whistle were sighing together in disappointment. Even that weak noise was heard through the rain and through the great expanse of nature. Instantly, like a startled flock of birds, the convicts flapped their wings twice and turned towards home.

There was not a dry place on us from head to foot. Like the Troop Leader's copper whistle, the cracks in our bones had been plugged with water. But consider how happy we were! Fate had decreed that we would have to work, but the old man in the sky had changed our fortune for that one day. While going from a drizzle to a downpour, the colours of the sky changed dramatically. The village in the distance, the fields, the wild wastes, the grasslands, the water in the canal all took on different hues as the weather changed. Behind the curtain of rain everything in life became less focused – so what were we racing back to do? Merely to plait straw ropes! Then why were we walking so fast? Let us stroll as if through a park!

It was then that Wang Sanyu and I began chatting, 'discussing literature and books'. He did not know much about Chinese poetry but said he liked the poetry of a particular Russia named Isakevsky. I asked why. He couldn't really answer – perhaps it was because many of the poems had been turned into songs and could easily be remembered. 'Listen to one,' he said, and he began to sing.

> 'A small winding road narrow and endless
> Going towards the vast unknown
> I want to follow this long narrow road
> Follow my love who is going to war . . .'

His singing voice had a deep timbre and was

extremely soulful. His vocal cords and lungs were sturdier than any whistle made of metal; hunger and rain had not reduced the coloration of the sound he produced. The tune was melodious and gentle; his voice was given added resonance by the humidity. It called back a remembrance of a world that had not completely vanished. And what was that world? Naturally it included a red flag and battle. It was world revolution, one class overpowering another, liberating all of mankind. It was for that sacred enterprise that we were here reforming ourselves, harvesting rice, making straw ropes, eating millet gruel. The sacred enterprise could not be a mistake. Surely it was we who were mistaken.

Although the thunderstorm raged and before us was an expanse of cold rain pounding a canal, kicking up countless bubbles on the frothing brown water, now our heads were uplifted. We were discussing Simenov's *Day and Night*. We were inspired, like the Red Army going to war. Stalingrad was ahead. Onward! For Stalin!

Wang Sanyu sang on, with deep emotion.

'When pear blossoms filled the horizon,
A light gauze hung over the river,
Kechousha moved along high steep banks,
The sound of her song like a radiant spring day.'

This song, too, was originally a poem by Isakevsky. I hadn't realized that Kechousha was not only a girl's name in Russian but also the name of the missile used by the Soviet Union to defend itself in war.

'And I always thought it was just the name of a woman,' I marvelled. Wang Sanyu went on to say that while the Russian Red Army loved Kechousha, it loved the missile's supremely intimidating strength even more.

It seems this was all written down in the book *Day and Night*.

We talked about contemporary Chinese novels, and about how inspirational some of the famous sayings in Russian novels were. We walked beside a canal so full it flowed even with the banks, like a river, and although we were wet through we didn't mind, like when you're wet after swimming and it doesn't matter. We were glowing with idealism. We recalled that phrase in *Advance the Mother Country*:

> 'Where could you ever find another country
> In which people have such freedom to come
>   and go?'

How could we imagine anything else? From childhood we were fed on illusory spiritual nourishment. A shining and resplendent and oh-so-desirable but unattainable future was spread before us. We weren't taught how to defend our own individual rights, how to distinguish where our real interests and where the people's interests lay. A massive orb of light was hung over our heads and we were made to understand that this was the purpose of our whole life's struggle. We seemed to have our sights set far in the distance, on the future of mankind – but the circle of light blinded our eyes. From the big yard of the labour reform camps to the fields, and back again from the fields to the big yard was the precisely defined path that we were permitted to travel. We were not even allowed to go to the other side of the canal.

And the villagers – what about their 'freedom'? I already knew that 'those who don't work hard will be sent to do labour reform', also that 'grass had already been dug clean by the local people'. Yet we truly did believe that sentence, 'Where could you ever find another country in which people have such freedom to come and go?'

Now, what country can you think of where people are really free?

The strange thing is that precisely because we thought we were being punished on behalf of an ideal, we did not feel that we were experiencing such great hardship. If it was to be millet gruel, all right, millet gruel. If we were to eat in the rain, fine, in the rain. Spiritual motivation and psychological deceit seem to be very much the same thing.

But it is hard to keep going for ever on sheer enthusiasm. As soon as he got home, Wang Sanyu lay down and when we went for food he was unable to get up. An attentive reader will notice that it was on that day in the diary that I got a second helping.

I am obliged to write about Wang Sanyu. Only by this can he know that he lived up to his ideal – that with only one life to live on earth, he sacrificed it to what he considered the most glorious enterprise on earth.

12 November

Stayed at home. In the morning the Old Commissar gave us Sick Numbers a lecture and criticized those who were eating greens. In the evening the men coming back from the fields were able to get hold of a lot of cabbages. The Troop Leader made a thorough search but he couldn't get them all. Head is dizzy, limbs have no energy. Heart pounds and breath comes in gasps. Whole body feels cold. This way for many days now. Today went to checkup at infirmary, doctor took my pulse, allowed me a full day's rest.

13 November

Rest all day. Used free time to write a report to the leaders reflecting the evil atmosphere in the troop, plan to give it to Troop Leader Zheng. Staying home uninteresting, nothing to do, but if I went out to work afraid I couldn't keep up with the others. Short of breath and no energy all day, getting food at noon I drew the smallest steamed bun. Very low in spirits.

18 November

The kitchen will serve only two meals a day starting today. One at nine o'clock in the morning, the other at four in the afternoon. We're getting so hungry we can't stand it. Coming back from work in the evenings the Small Group is eating raw grass. On the 15th we got a stove inside the Number, so now everybody fights for it to be able to cook their greens. They hit each other and fight just to get some fire for cooking. Fang Aihua stole some of Dai Haixi's lotus flowers and ate them.

I was able to get some cabbage roots, cooked them directly over the flame and ate them, very tasty. But two sweet potatoes were confiscated by Troop Leader Zheng.

25 November

Again Canal Twenty-two in the morning. The groups were reorganized into two-hour, four-hour, six-hour and complete-rest groups. I was assigned to a two-hour group, which was group Five in Agricultural Troop Two. We are to work only two hours each day. The Group Leader was to be Tan Pingwu; Tan wouldn't do it so they sent Zhu Zhenbang again. Kitchen now divided into four 'stoves': an agricultural work stove, a four-and-six-hour stove, a Sick Numbers' stove and a cadres' stove. Our two-hour group is to eat at the Sick Number's stove. Dizzy every day, reeling, no energy. Yesterday ate a number of sweet potatoes, taken when I helped push the cart. The rest were confiscated last night.

Blood in my phlegm when I got up. By chance saw a copy of *Ningxia News*. On the third page was an article on the Old Commissar and in it were many sentences that came from 'Shine on Crimson Rays'.* The author was noted as someone named Wang. Never mind, my efforts weren't for nothing.

1 December

No energy day after day. Too tired to write. Worth recording that these days we all had checkups several times, probably because they're again reorganizing the groups. My weight is 101 jin, blood pressure 110/80, temperature 36.1 degrees.

Got weighed with cotton-padded clothes and shoes on, but am still much heavier than the eighty-eight jin I was before. Comforting. Met Su Ruixin at the door of the infirmary. He ran away once. Said he'd do it again if he had the chance. 'If you can just get food on the Outside, it's much better than in here.'

5 December

They announced the start of the winter regimen. Demanded that the system be tightened up, that everything be done on time (although serving meals, of course, is never on time). Every evening we are to study documents on the system. Troop Leader Zheng distributed more paper, told each of us to write accusations of others. Heh Zhiyun criticized me in the meeting, said the way I traded material possessions for something to eat was a question of principle.

20 December

Chaotic these last few days, nothing to record. The leaders' searches and investigations are very strict but greens and sweet potatoes are still being boiled in the evenings. Has become a regular practice: things that individuals bring in are distributed to those with some energy left in them. In the day they distributed some sweet potatoes to me but in the evening Tan Pingwu and Zhu Zhenbang took them and ate them themselves. This infuriated me. Received a package from Mother, again nothing to eat in it. Mama's letter said that post offices in Beijing and Shanghai are strictly controlled,

---

* Article written by the author in praise of the Old Commissar.

not allowed to mail any food. Old Wang returned from the State Farm at Jian Quan, is now staying in the Peasants and Workers Troop. I used my full-rest day to go and see him. Health very bad, does not look as if he'll be alive for long. He gave me a pinch of salt and heated a little leftover rice for me to eat. I gave him some old clothes.

Will soon be New Year's. They want each of us groups to write a guarantee. Guarantee to have a safe, happy New Year.

China may be inept at learning good things from other countries, but we are just as hopeless when it comes to emulating bad things. For example, in terms of convict management, the labour camps in China in the 1960s were much more lenient than the camps in the former Soviet Union and Eastern Europe. (I regard the famine situation throughout China and the management of labour reform camps as two separate issues.)

This is not to say that the highest levels of authority in China were not interested in imitating the Soviet Union's gulag. Indeed they hoped to move the entire system intact to China, together with its methods of control. They intended to use it to deal with the class enemies in China's own prisons. In the 1950s, the understanding in our country was that we must study from Big Brother and that we must study well. This meant maintaining an attitude of submission and humility. The political systems of Russia and China were similar, as were the philosophical beliefs of Stalin and Mao. But even if Chinese authorities were so humble that they bowed right down to the ground, they soon ran into two key problems:

1. They lacked the material conditions to implement a rigorous system of control.
2. They lacked the human resources for a wholesale importation of Big Brother Russia's gulag system.

Material resources

To reach the former Soviet Union's standards in managing its gulag, all the cement and steel in China would not have been able to handle the needs of labour camps set up from the 1950s to the late 1970s.

Fortunately, China has always used wood and earth as primary building materials. Even the palaces of emperors were made of wood, brick and tiles. Buildings were not meant to be made of metal – the most sacred and elegant of all, the Temple of Heaven in Beijing, wasn't allowed to use a scrap of metal. A nail in such a structure was out of the question. How could a mere prison for incarcerating convicts think of transgressing ancient rules? This is one reason few buildings are left to posterity in China, from luxurious palaces down to simple dark prisons.

Europe is different. There one can see many sites that kings, aristocrats and prisoners have occupied in the past, ancient walls that were made of enduring stone, great gates that were cast of iron or bronze. In China, people were accustomed to using primitive buildings made of impermanent blocks of earth to lock up prisoners. The Chinese locked inside would never have dreamed of denying that they were prisoners just because the buildings did not look like prisons.

By the latter part of the 1950s, when the labour reform population was greatly increased, some of the camps were so crude that they looked like nothing more than impoverished villages. There were no steel fences, no guard dogs, nothing but a few soldiers with guns wandering back and forth. Afterwards, by the time of the Great Cultural Revolution, any place would do as a prison: an office, a dormitory, a horse stable, a pigpen. It got to the point that the captors would just draw a circle on the ground and declare that men should stay inside. And the prisoners complied – they never dared cross this imaginary minefield by so much as a step. Thought control came to be used as the main material for construction. If Stalin could have seen this method of building prisons, I believe he would have been ashamed of his own meagre accomplishments.

The wall around the labour reform state farm where I spent two periods of my life was made of earth – it could have been pushed over by a few men uniting their efforts. The front gate was nailed together from a few planks of wood; the bark on the sides of the boards had never been planed off. Like convicts, this gate seemed forever to be listing in a state of near collapse and it groaned whenever it was opened or shut. We convicts had never seen its lock, for this was on the outside and the gate was locked at night. By morning when we went to work the lock had been taken away by a Troop Leader. I assume it was made of metal but it must have been a cheap device – a pair of pliers could probably have snapped it in two.

In winter we convicts were always complaining that the doors to each Number were so flimsy that the slightest puff of wind could find its way inside. The walls of the Numbers were *gandalei* walls, made of earthern blocks. The foundation was just two layers of bricks. In half an hour's time a rat could easily find a way to wriggle inside. None the less, rarely did anyone try to escape. In such 'prisons' they were able to lock men securely away.

Standards of hygiene in China were similarly lower than those one is accustomed to reading about in Russian camps. In the two periods I was in camps, one of which was for seven years, I rarely took a bath or changed my underwear. Sometimes you could watch your underclothes dancing with motion, as though a gentle breeze was blowing the pages of a newspaper. When you peeled off your trousers you found your body crawling with lice.

The leaders never dreamed of issuing any kind of delousing solution. In the summer, all you could do was take off your clothes to sleep: 'let the damned lice starve for the night!' In the winter you could strip and hang all your clothes out in the big yard – in twenty below zero temperatures (C), the lice would freeze to death. But the brief interval of sleep was insufficient to kill off all the life-clinging little eggs. The next day when you put your clothes on, the temperature of your body would be ideal for hatching out a whole new generation of lice. Often more would spring forth than had just frozen to death. And so, when one wasn't busy doing other things, one picked out lice. As soon as you got one the practice was to pop it in your mouth. Chewing on lice and lice eggs is rather like crunching sesame seeds – both are tasty and make a crispy sound.

All things considered, lice are a kind of meat, rich in protein. When one's hunger is intolerable, stuffing lice in the mouth can relieve the craving for food. Sometimes when I have observed lice closely with these thoughts in mind, I have found that strings of lice eggs can be quite appealing – they glisten like tiny pearls or not yet fully ripe grapes. They may well be the treat of the future.

You cannot blame the authorities of the labour reform camp for the problem of lice. Eradicating lice is actually quite simple, but the fact is that the leaders of the camps did not and had never had the concept that lice were to be got rid of. To a peasant's way of thinking, a man whose body was not covered with lice was a man not far from death.

When the leaders talked to us about hygiene, our Old Commissar preached as follows: 'Having a few lice is nothing to worry about! Man's blood is hot, that's why lice like to feed on it! Lice on the body prove a man's blood is still warm, that he's healthy! Why, even the Emperor had a few imperial lice! You've never seen what lice do? A person dies, his blood cools off . . . lice will crawl off his body of their own accord! So you must be careful! A man who isn't raising lice on his body has blood that's turning cold! No need to go to a doctor. I can tell he's got some terrible disease!'

There is no historical record as to whether or not the Emperor had lice, but I have heard this from more than just the Old Commissar. Among peasant cadres it was regarded as established fact. Lice were a way of measuring the state of a man's health – together with leeches they were a kind of medical diagnostic tool. Our Troop Leaders, Camp Leader, and Station Leader including the Old Commissar himself truly believed that not until they itched so much that it was unbearable should they voluntarily delouse themselves. We convicts often watched as they called evening rollcall or made reports, clawing at and scratching bodies as inflamed as our own. I have personally seen the Old Commissar pull a small thing from under his collar, squint at it a moment and then toss it in his mouth.

In terms of administrative procedures, again China lags far behind Russia in documenting its prisoners. In Russia, at least then, our understanding was that every convict had a relatively complete file on his case. It way typed out and accompanied by a photograph. To

Chinese convicts such documentation would have seemed a compliment to the prisoner. Hard, high-quality paper, words typed out with a typewriter – this deluxe treatment might have made more bearable the minor detail that one had never committed the crime.

In 1958, when I first went into the camps, all we were given was a piece of the most primitive kind of paper made from rice stalks. Only my name had been hand-written on the paper – everything else was a printed form. There were, for example, no personalized details about which laws I might have contravened. What's more, the words were so poorly printed that they were nearly illegible. The paper was flimsy and irregular – you felt you'd better hurry and hand it over to the prison authorities or it might be damaged and then you would be in serious trouble. You would be someone with an unclear past. Lack of information on you would allow anyone who wanted you put away to fabricate your past.

Laws cannot be enforced when the most basic material conditions are lacking. Never mind that there were no laws in the first place, and don't for a moment think that leaders were going to pass a detailed set of laws restraining *themselves*. As a result, the documents of convicts who were locked up in prisons or pressed into camps were often either non-existent or completely mixed up. When rightists started being rehabilitated in 1979, after convicts had raised their appeals and been thoroughly investigated, it was discovered that many had never been capped as rightists at all. They had been wrongly incarcerated for more than twenty years, and quite apart from the waste of lifetimes, there was absolutely no compensation. Nothing to show for it at all.

Some people had died but were still living according to their files. Others were living but the files said they were dead The spot where a convict's photograph should have been was generally blank – photographic equipment was not widespread. There was no written material explaining what a convict was supposed to look like – the traditional practice of describing a convict's appearance had long since disappeared. There was no way the administration of a camp could match case documents with an actual person, so frequently you had a Mr Li taking the place of a Mr Zhang, the one committing the crime of the other and vice versa.

China has many people with the same proper and given name – if you were confused with someone else, you might be dragged through hell. Your entire life history could be revised. You could become the son of others, have been through things you had never experienced at all, be made to have done things you would never even dream of doing. And it was unacceptable if you didn't confess to everything, for there was no way to go back and find your true self and explain. Obstruction of the people's justice was an additional crime.

I was born in 1936, but when I came out of the camps the second time in 1968 my release authorization said that I had been born in 1938. I could not, of course, demand those two years back. People would have ignored me. If I explained things poorly, the commune I went to would have begun to have doubts about me: what does this nut want to be born two years earlier for, anyway? What's he have in mind? What political angle is he trying to prove?

The lack of such basic physical things as uniforms, paper and so on meant that class distinctions between management cadres and prisoners were not obvious. This not only softened the most severe regulations that the highest authorities would have liked to carry out, but was one of the reasons people were willing to stay alive under the pressure. Chinese have always been a nation that does not mind poverty but cannot stand inequality.

For example, it is true that the Old Commissar may have been eating a duck a day but he could only enjoy it in secret, by himself. He could not eat it openly before other cadres; and this special privilege definitely did not extend to his family. I learned this from the convict who guarded the vegetable cellar. The Old Commissar was getting on in years when he married, probably because he had served in the army and never had the chance before. By the time he approached sixty he was still surrounded by a flock of children who depended on him. His wife was a Shaanxi girl who often went to the vegetable cellar with the wives of other cadres to get their vegetables. Like the family members of other cadres she, too, would have to be nice to the convict who guarded the food, ask him to slide the measure a little further over on his measuring pole, and so on. The clever devil of a guard quickly made friends with this wife of a high-ranking official. One time the wife frankly discussed her problems with him: lots of children at home, nobody getting enough to eat, each just trying to grow a little bigger, makes a mother ache to see them . . . can you help, etc.

The guard instantly replied in a most generous manner. 'Of course! Just let me know whenever you're having trouble. I'll do my best. I don't have any grain here but I do have vegetables . . . whenever you want

I'll send some over. I'm just worried that if the Old Commissar were to know he'd never forgive me. If you can keep it quiet I'll bring some over every day.'

The woman said, 'Don't send them over in daylight. I'd trouble you to have them sent under cover of darkness. And don't call out to the old man when you come – I'll leave the gate open so you can just throw them inside. That would be fine. If you don't make any noise, how's he to know who sent the food?'

So the guard hauled a hemp bag full of vegetables over to the Old Commissar's house that very night. When he got to the front gate he found that it was indeed left open for him. The Old Commissar was resting on the kang inside and yelled, 'Who's there?' They had already put out the light and it was dark inside the house. Instead of keeping quiet the guard intentionally called in a loud voice. 'It's me! Bringing some vegetables.' He threw the hemp bag down inside the gate.

The next day, the woman came by to thank him, her eyes glistening with gratitude.

'Did the Old Commissar say anything?' he asked.

'Say anything!' she replied. 'Aren't those his children as well? He's happy too when they get a few more bites to eat.' From then on the guard took over a hemp bag of vegetables every few days and helped the Old Commissar raise those children. According to him there were five boys and girls, of all sizes. The biggest had just entered middle school, the smallest had just entered primary school, 'every one of them skinny as a monkey. They scarcely put down their bowls when they're hungry for more.'

That was the way the household of a high-ranking official got its food. The cabbage and potatoes were cooked in a pot of hot water. The most they threw in was a pinch of salt, certainly no meat.

In general, I have to say that in terms of what cadres and convicts got to eat and drink there was some disparity in quantity but not much in quality. We picked out the grass roots, they could eat the grass above the roots. That was about it.

On the 25th of November I wrote in the diary, 'the kitchen was divided into four stoves: the Peasant-and-Workers' stove, the four-and-six-hour stove, the Sick Numbers' stove and the cadres' stove.' This was to say that the cadres' stove was set up in the big kitchen, too. Cadres benefited by having their stove together with ours, since they could take some of our rations. But they still could not get hold of any other kind of food.

As for clothes, although convicts in the camps wore patched rags, the quality of the fabric was often better than the fabric of cadres' uniforms. Cadres had never even heard of the worsted or tweed of other fabrics that some intellectuals wore. People now poor who once experienced privileged lives are, in the eyes of Chinese, worthy of intense envy. It is no wonder that when they mentioned that KMT general he was always 'the one with the golden-haired monkey jacket'. Even Troop Leaders regarded a man with clothes as somebody.

The Public Security apparatus was supposed to be the machinery that kept the nation going. Belt-tightening was belt-tightening, and revolutionary spirit was preserved, but when the cadres appeared before the masses in rags it must be admitted that the prestige of the nation was diminished. Prisoners were terrified of Troop Leaders, but what they feared were the ropes in their hands, or being docked a ladle of gruel, or that they would instigate other convicts to use sadistic means of having them photographed. Other than that, leaders did not enjoy a shred of prestige in our eyes. When someone ordering you around is dressed no better than a beggar, why should you be afraid?

Appearance is important. People's perceptions depend initially on how you look. If bosses look shabby, how can you respect them? Why should you stand up straight and remove your hat when you see one, shout 'report' before entering a door, not sit down until told to sit down? In Chinese labour reform camps, at least for the time that I was there, such formalities did not exist. When we saw officials we slouched by them without so much as an acknowledgement.

None the less, the rags we wore, the weeds we ate, everything in China was illuminated by the shining glory of the person of Chairman Mao. Without the radiant light emanating from Mao Zedong, the country would soon have been revealed as nothing more than a pile of rotten garbage. Who was 'the country'? Other than the distinguished Chairman Mao, nobody could claim to represent this concept. Beneath the overpowering brilliance of those shining rays, the status of everyone else paled to insignificance. During the Great Cultural Revolution, dragging lesser dignitaries out to struggle against was fine: go ahead. If you said you wanted to rectify them to death: fine, go ahead. They had lost the lustre of their own identities, and as a result common people had no more regard for them than dirt. All the glory and luminosity was concentrated in the person of Chairman Mao. There may never before have been a social system that brought such pressure and impoverishment to bear on a country's citizens in such equal measure.

Human resources

The second difficulty authorities faced in attempting a wholesale importation of the gulag archipelago of Big Brother Russia was that of inadequate human resources. Using political terminology, the quality of our cadres was inadequate. Cadres were mainly born of peasant stock. They had no education or technical training. It was impossible for them to have effective control of any kind of tightly structured, scientific management system. They certainly lacked the necessary skills for managing large numbers of convicts in a labour reform camp.

After 1979, the majority of political prisoners were rehabilitated. For many years, China had seized hundreds of thousands of people in political movements. Some were thrown into jail or camps many times – I was arrested five times in succession. Now history has produced evidence that these people were wrongly arrested: but can it be that China at the time had no truly bad people? Of course there were bad people; it was just that 'cadres of inadequate material to be cadres' could not be arrested. The truly bad people were those arresting the others.

If the gulag archipelago is considered to be the iron-clad system of a socialist state, then what we imitated and brought into China was a clay replica. I have already said that the system was greatly 'softened' in the process, by which I meant that it looked huge and imposing but had cracks in it. One could hide amongst these cracks. If your standards were not too high, you could even feel fairly well off. If it hadn't been for the calamity of a nationwide famine, the labour camps could have served as a convenient and fairly adequate retreat for riding out the storm of the Fifties, Sixties and Seventies in China. Compared to being subjected to daily criticism and judgement in outside society, they were a relatively safe place to spend your time. In fact, in those days labour reform camps were a place many people longed to be.

I naturally look at this from the standpoint of one who was locked up inside a camp. I cannot see it from the perspective of the highest authorities. If I had been a high authority and pretended to be a convict in order to come into the camps to do reconnaissance, I would have been furious at what I found there. I would have cursed the cadres for their lenience, for not carrying out the high-pressure reform tactics I had ordered.

The main reason the system was a pale shadow of the Russian gulag was that those administering the system were a bunch of peasants. Although Chinese peasants have their shortcomings and are fundamentally unsuited to managing large institutions, by intuition alone they have a good sense of what is real and what is not. They could not grasp an idealized or formalized approach to 'truth' as represented by communist ideology, but they were generally well endowed with a sense of humanity. Even as they scorned intellectuals, they admired them. The emotions were very complex. They could swallow the concept fed to them by the authorities that these people were class enemies of the state, but when faced with an actual person, any hypothetical crime evaporated. It was obvious that we were nothing but shrivelled, famished racks of skin-covered bones. When the peasants saw us, the dire warnings of the authorities dissolved into pity. The humanity of Chinese peasants, and indeed of all Chinese, is a strong acid. It can corrode to a pile of rust the most rigidly constructed set of rules.

In short, those administering the camps were also human and were also poor. It took half a day for some of them to plan how to smoke a cigarette: should I smoke it now, or endure a while longer, or should I wait until after I've eaten? After making up their minds they would smoke to the very end, when burnt fingers could no longer hold a cigarette and had to let it fall. (I have observed this phenomenon rather closely.) Their treatment of convicts might still include beating and cursing, violent and painful treatment, but other than a small number of truly crazy cadres most of them did not do this voluntarily. After all, there was great pressure on them, too. They had to represent themselves well to their own bosses.

I say this not in order to exonerate or forgive them. My evaluation stems from a clear, cold analysis of what happened later. Certain cadres later become local emperors – warlords or dictators of certain regions. By then they were capable of any evil. But their shift in character had to be formed under specific social conditions and historical events – a fundamental change requires a catalytic agent, and this agent was the Great Cultural Revolution. In the 1960s, the character of these people had not yet been warped too much. At that time they were still like little lice eggs – only after a gestation period nurtured by the warmth of the Great Leader's body during the Great Cultural Revolution did they develop into real lice.

On 12 November, the Old Commissar assembled the Sick Numbers who had stayed in the camp and not gone out to work. The ration of grain was continually being lowered and the number of sick and dying was increasing. As a result, almost all of those who had not died had become Sick Numbers. In order to cling to life, Sick Numbers now stole anything they could find to eat: grass from the open fields, leaves from trees, vegetable roots, rats, toads, lice. It is said that in many regions the local people went out to dig a kind of white-coloured earth to eat.

In the 1960s in China, the scope of what mankind deems edible expanded considerably – the period was a vast experiment in testing the limits of what can be included in the category 'food'. This was a major contribution of the Great Leader to mankind. The labour reform authorities knew perfectly well that the deaths were due to lack of nutrition, but they did not dare question a single line of the regulations regarding grain distribution. At that time, no one in China dared make even a small farting peep about this very sensitive subject. Marshal Peng Dehuai had already served as a lesson: we saw his cart overturned in the road before us.

And yet they saw piles of convicts dying before them every day – some reason other than grain and food had to be found to explain it. The labour reform camp leaders studied this up and down and finally found an explanation. It turned out the reason convicts were dying so briskly was not because they ate too little but because they ate too much!

Superficially, this seemed persuasive. When you think about it, eating whatever you can grab onto, cooked or raw, poisonous or dirty or full of bacteria, goes counter to all man's habits since he graduated from being an ape. We exceeded the absorptive capacity of our intestines, which had been developing gradually in the other direction for a long time. (Most regrettably, in such a short period the intestines of Chinese could not accommodate themselves to the policy of the Great Leader – this was blamed, not on the policy, but on the slow reactions of Chinese digestive organs.) After instituting the lowered-rations-to-be-substituted-with-gourds-and-greens policy, the first phenomenon was not famished people but universal intestinal disorders.

All the logic was on the side of the leaders. You could not point to a single person as evidence of death from starvation. In fact, the initial symptoms of the great majority of convicts who died were vomiting, diarrhoea and swelling up, then panting breath, then a near-death struggle. What would one do in the course of that struggle? As before, go out to steal things to eat! Roots, wild grasses, rats, toads, that sort of thing – no matter how much anti-diarrhoea medicine the doctors administered and how much anti-inflammatory medicine, it was no use. In the end convicts would have severe diarrhoea, become dehydrated, and die.

How could it be that there was inadequate nutrition? We were most fortunate to be living in the Mao Zedong era; we were bathed in his nourishing light. Our lives were different from the old society; we were in the process of striding into the paradise of communism. How could we go around creating rumours about nutrition being inadequate!

It seems your head has insufficient nutrition in it! Excuse me, you still need a bit of study. Better send you to do hard labour to be reformed!

Labour reform authorities were clearer than your average person about the consequences of saying the wrong things, and so they called doctors in to do a little research. After the research they knew that swelling could be attributed to a number of causes and they selected the most convenient conclusions. Those convicts who died after swelling up had died because they ate too much salt. Those convicts who had died but were not swollen up had died as a result of eating overly large quantities of greens.

Salt was selected as the cause of the swelling problem. But remember that convicts had worked hard to get their greens. They might have stolen a clutch of vegetable leaves from the workfields, or expended the energy of nine cows and two tigers in catching a rat, or suffered the terrors of hell in taking a sweet potato. In short, they had with great difficulty got together some raw materials to boil up in plain water for a meal – how could you tell them not to take a little enjoyment in a pinch of salt?!

Try it yourself. Cook a pot of water and throw in some roots or leaves. Don't use any salt or seasoning at all, and then try to eat it. You will find that a bowl of tasteless grass, even to starving people near death, turns the stomach. People have advanced from the stage of being monkeys; their tongues have been trained to be selective. Having something to eat is not enough – they want flavour. It is hard to return to a stage of eating like a wild animal, putting your mouth straight against a tree or the ground and chewing.

And so after food and tobacco the next most important thing that we searched for in the camp was salt. For better or worse, the labour reform camp still served two meals a day; putting lots of salt in a bowl of millet gruel made it into a 'dish' according to the Chinese way of eating. Even if you impulsively wanted to throw back your gruel in one gulp you would restrain yourself, sip it slowly and so prolong the pleasure of eating, much in the way that a man tries to prolong the pleasure of sex.

You can't help but admire the abilities of the Great Leader for administering the country in such a way that in those years even the most fundamental, inexpensive daily necessity, the manufacture of which was supremely easy, was declared to be in critically short supply throughout the country. I have read a certain amount of Chinese history, and at times extremely remote mountainous areas inhabited by ethnic minorities lacked enough edible salt, but in the entire Twenty-four Histories I have not found a record of the country lacking cooking salt on a universal basis. And yet this strange aberration occurred in China in the twentieth century.

Don't panic! Under astute and brilliant leadership, we have ways to conquer all difficulties! If greens and gourds can replace grain, cooking salt can of course be replaced with other things.

The first approach was to use a low-grade inferior salt. We were given large quantities of mineral salt that had not been processed in any way and that was mixed with other things. This grey material was composed of some lumps that were as large as a fist, and that were so hard that you could have cracked a man's skull with them. Villagers would buy it and take it home, then have to spend all their energy grinding it down to irregular chunks the size of rice grains. It was hard to get these to dissolve in a wok. When you had cooked your vegetables, the vegetables were vegetables, the grains of salt were still grains of salt – when you'd finished eating you could pick them off the plate and use them again.

Later, the authorities pushed a kind of soy sauce paste onto the market. This was a seasoning that suddenly flooded the entire country. Soy sauce paste was said to have been made by the most advanced, most scientific methods. After concentrating soy sauce it was again refined and processed so that from a liquid you ended up with a dark-brown crystalline solid. This was declared to be a distillation of soy sauce and was given the name Soy Sauce Essence.

Chinese have always revered this word 'essence'. Whatever has become an essence is to be desired. Like *wei-jing*,* all you needed was to put a little pinch in whatever you were eating and it would miraculously have a delicious salty flavour. A little pinch of Soy Sauce Essence was much better than a large block of mineral salt.

Soy sauce paste . . . soy sauce essence . . . soy sauce essence . . . soy sauce paste . . . – this was truly a life-enhancing mantra. At the beginning only convicts coming in from the Outside possessed this miraculous Essence. A piece of Essence could be traded for a wrist-watch. Not long after, the camp store began to have it for sale. It was wrapped in grass-paper and was about as big as a paperback book; packages of it were lined up like volumes on the previously empty racks for display. The price was now quite low, just in line with

* Literally 'flavour-essence', also known as MSG.

convicts' purchasing power. Think how incredibly excited we were to get hold of the essential essence of something edible. This material had no dregs or roughage or other inedible material in it; all of it could be absorbed by the body.

Convicts began to dissolve this material in water and drink it in quantity. You'd take a small piece of Soy Sauce Essence and put it in hot water, stir it around, and it instantly turned into a bowl of slightly flavoured light-brown soy sauce soup. If you could manage to steal a sprig of green onion it was even more marvellous. You would chug it down and the stomach would immediately swell, but at least the feeling of hunger would abate for a while. The labour reform camps did not in fact ration water, so in time convicts began to drink this soup all day long. They drank it until their stomachs got bigger and bigger, until their internal cavaties were like a bag that hung down, so that when they walked they gurgled like a water cart bumping along an uneven road. After swelling they would continue to drink and then their skin would begin to crack; their four limbs and stomachs, even their faces, would begin to ooze a yellow-coloured excretion. When you continue to blow air into a balloon that has been overextended, it will eventually explode. In this case, overconsumption truly was the cause of the death of many convicts.

If it had not been for Soy Sauce Essence, after so many intervening years I would not have remembered the lecture that the Old Commissar gave us on 12 November.

The spit flew around him as he yelled, 'So what's this soy sauce paste? They even say it's the essence of soy sauce! Humph! That stuff is pure and simple opium. It's exactly identical to opium. You all realize that? Opium is also called paste; it's also boiled down from a liquid; from a white syrup you boil it till it turns black. In the old society, back when people wanted to commit suicide they'd swallow a piece as big as a fingernail and their legs would buckle! You say that's poisonous or not?! Right now you're all eating this soy sauce paste all day; it's no different from smoking opium! You're addicted to it! You're eating so much a lot of you have swollen up! Died! Don't you see it? You still don't know it's something that's bad for people . . . !'

The Sick Numbers who had been called in to listen to this lecture gathered in the big yard of the labour reform camp. Some were sitting, some lying down like black pigeons covering the ground. The doctors had been given notice by the camp authorities that they should not restrict the number of people they allowed to be Sick Numbers. Even if convicts had no obvious symptoms and were merely weak, they should be permitted not to work. Faced with a population of enfeebled men, even a specialist in quantitative analysis could not have come up with a more astute decision. On this particular day I noticed that the number of men staying at home was pretty much equal to the entire population of the camp.

The Old Commissar had by now adopted a policy of one eye open one eye shut with regard to how convicts listened to his reports. In 1958, convicts had to stand to respectful attention. The next year they were allowed to sit on the ground, but were not allowed to lower their heads and think their own thoughts, nor were they allowed to whisper to each other. Now, many Sick Numbers were stretched out on the ground, taking up the space of three or four men, so that the entire yard had become one great bed. At a glance, it looked as though the ranks of convicts had swelled to several times their original number.

Give convicts an inch and they will take a mile. They were now taking advantage of this permission to sleep on the ground by emphasizing their various ailments. Those with lung disease in particular were coughing like crazy, to the point that the Old Commissar had to shout to be heard over their thunderous hacking.

The Old Commissar's message was negative, but what he was talking about was Soy Sauce Essence, which was much more interesting than the usual lecture. You could lie down and sleep, you could cough, you could fart, you could close your eyes and pick your nose, be as comfortable as you liked. The evening light was particularly fine that day. Listening to him excoriate this Essence in his unique language under the open sky was as entertaining as listening to an actor perform a soliloquy.

Some of the words in his lecture have had an irreversible influence on the way I live my life today.

He said, 'Haven't you noticed? The ones who drink soy sauce soup are the ones who die! What is that stuff made of? It is made of chemicals! Nothing made of chemicals is any good! These days the whole country is yelling about promoting the use of chemical fertilizers! I say our farm should resist to the end and not use them! Keep on using farmhouse fertilizer and wet green compost to fertilize the ground! Chemical fertilizers, made from chemical processes – why, you put them on a patch of ground and it gets hard! It turns a perfectly good piece of earth into a rock! Don't you think that because this year's harvest looks pretty good, next year will be good! Dog's day! Next year that land won't be growing a single sprout! Why? Chemicals take the dirt and burn it out! You tell me, is chemistry powerful or not? On this earth, what is tougher than dirt?!'

He stomped firmly on the ground several times with his foot, so that the earth in the big yard resounded with a thud, indicating that the earth was indeed comparably durable.

'But, even dirt this tough is afraid of fertilizer made from chemicals! You tell me, is that odd? Things made from chemicals – there's not one that isn't hot-natured! It will either burn something right away or it will burn it slowly! Tell me, which of you has a stomach and intestines that are more durable than this earth? Tell me! You tell me!'

He used his stubby finger to point at the sitting, sleeping, lying Sick Numbers in turn, asking which man had innards more resilient than the earth.

'Nobody! Of course!'

He now let out a happy, crafty smile, having achieved complete victory in his logic. 'Yes! Whose innards can win over the earth! If chemicals burn the earth, they'll certainly burn out the dog's innards of every one of you!'

The idea that this kind of chemical product was 'hot-natured', that it could hurt a man's insides, made a strong impression on me. When convicts went crazy drinking this Soy Sauce Essence in quantity, I did not indulge. My philosophy was, 'Rather have one mouthful of immortal's elixir than a crate of sodden mashed pears.' I am not fond of drinking water or soup, and when it comes to eating and drinking I am a materialist

– only if it is something solid that I can chew on do I have the sense of eating something real. Even vegetable roots or fermenting vegetable leaves were better to me than flavourful Soy Sauce Essence.

After his lecture I was even less willing to buy Soy Sauce Essence to dissolve in hot water. I did not eat 'chemical' products while working at the labour reform camp, or later working on the Outside, nor later yet when I was rehabilitated and became an editor, then an author. Indeed, to this day I am extremely careful about not eating synthetic food. I do my best not to eat MSG. If I can't tell whether or not a given foodstuff being sold in a store has preservatives, colouring agents, etc., I don't buy it. Somehow, the minute I see on the packaging that food or drink has a chemical additive I immediately think of 'fire' which leads me to think of 'hot-natured', and the possibility that after eating or drinking the stomach will be slowly burned.

Who would have thought that the Old Commissar's theory, regarded at the time as crazy and backward, would become so fashionable. It seems it was very much in accord with scientific analysis of what we should eat and drink. In China, only wealthy people can be picky about what they eat and can avoid eating anything but 'green' or organic food. In our markets today, there is scarcely any meat or vegetable that does not have chemical pollutants, so that knowledgeable people are making a great uproar about the side effects. They want to return to the planting policies of the Old Commissar and strictly control the application of chemicals. Our Old Commissar was a pioneer in China in the 1960s in trying to preserve the natural environment as well as the internal environment of the human organism.

It has occurred to me, for I did spend twenty-two years in the camps, that while I was given some training in good behaviour there (for example, this guidance on food from the Old Commissar), I was more thoroughly steeped in bad habits. I learned things that are standard to convicts: a sense of servility, craftiness, a dead-pan face, a thick skin. I also developed an ability to listen to fate, or accept fate, and with it a contradictory awareness of how man's actions can conquer, and perhaps destroy, nature. All good and bad things influence me without my knowing it. They are not susceptible to my direction. The good things are beneficial to me but the bad things are hard for me to change. I am what I am – I have been reformed into being this kind of person. I fear that this may be true of the world in general. As Hegel said, the world advances in a spiral pattern – man's experiences repeat themselves in new forms. One hopes that the anti-rightist movement and the Cultural Revolution will not be among those that return.

As for Soy Sauce Essence, when the lowered-rations policy ended, this commodity disappeared from the market. They had claimed it was made with the most advanced scientific methods – why should such a marvellous thing cease to be promoted? As it turned out, it was only a synthetic substance made from inferior salt, chemicals and colouring agents. Exactly as the Old Commissar had said, it was bad for human health. But during the lowered-rations period the country took no responsibility for selling it to the masses as good food.

On the day he lectured us on this subject, the Old Commissar was unusually lenient in his criticism of those of us who ate greens, stole vegetables, picked leaves, and caught small animals. He said a number of things that I don't remember clearly, but there was one sentence that came close to being a folk saying: 'Greens belong to the general public, but your stomachs belong to yourselves!'

What he meant was that the camps, nationally managed labour reform troops, were not upset about letting go of a little publicly owned property such as greens. Trying to get convicts not to steal these things was in order to ensure their own good health.

'How much can you eat?' he demanded. 'If you don't eat these things, won't they just go rotten in the ground anyway? Or become garbage to be thrown away? Our leaders really are afraid you'll destroy your stomachs! Greens belong to the general public, but your stomachs belong to yourselves! I'm telling you, the loss of a few vegetables won't make us that poor, the country won't be ruined, but you ruin your stomachs and it's going to change your life! Your families are still hoping you're going to come home! So maybe you'll go home, but if you have a busted gut and hang around all day as a burden – what about that?

'You all love to eat greens: starting tomorrow, we're telling the kitchen to cook the greens you're going to bring them! They'll cook them up for a minute in the pot before they give you gruel and greens back together.'

He had not said a word about adding grain to our diet, but the convicts heard in this news the hint of additional food.

This proclamation, stemming not from any desire to preserve the nation's wealth but from a considered judgement of what was in our best interests, struck a very deep chord. Even those sleeping on the ground were moved and raised their sick bodies up on one arm to listen.

But we soon found that the food being slopped in our bowls by the cook was not a particle more than it had ever been. Putting the convict's greens in the big pot for a moment and stirring them around until cooked meant very little – what came back was exactly one ladle, no more no less. Moreover, in order to carry out the instructions that we were to get no more salt, the cooks stopped putting any salt at all into our millet gruel.

This change in the system had only one virtue so far as convicts were concerned. It kept the gruel from getting as thin as water. When salt was added to the wooden buckets, the more the cooks stirred the gruel the thinner it became. I remember one cook who, in order to be absolutely even-handed about his portion, would stir twice for every time he dished out a ladle. Back bent, head down, he would open his arms wide in a great arc, like a phoenix opening his wings. He would swish two large circles in the great bucket, then ladle one bowl's worth of soup, stand up and hand it to the convict. Down would go his head and back, and the dance-like movement would start again. Serve a ladle, stir two ladles, serve a ladle, stir two ladles. The wooden bucket would resound with the regularity of a metronome. The rhythm seemed beautiful to us – each of us was secure in the knowledge of getting a fair portion of food. The cook was well intentioned, for he surely put more energy into this performance than he would otherwise have used. But, the more he stirred the thinner the gruel became.

Without salt, this process went the other way. Now

the more the cooks stirred, the thicker the gruel became.
As the bucket cooled off the gruel would become a nice
thick paste. If the cook's hand hesitated for a moment
over the bowl as he was pouring a serving, the con-
gealed gruel at the bottom of the ladle would slide into
the convict's bowl as well. And if there happened to be
a long cooked leaf that stuck to the outside of the ladle,
the cook would consider that the property of the next
lucky convict – he would slop it onto the convict's bowl.
Stuck half in, half out, like a line of green snot, this
precious leaf would even be nicely coated with millet
gruel!

Why did we still get only that one ladleful, even
though the Old Commissar had said that our vegetable
roots and leaves were to be added to, not substituted
for, our millet gruel? The cooks had the answer.

'Stop dreaming! You want to slurp a ladle of millet
gruel and also eat a ladle of vegetables! How lovely!
Since you've eaten those vegetables what do you think
they are eating in town? Right now villagers are depending on these same greens to stay alive! Where's this
coming from? It's out of the mouths of farmers!'

It turned out the townspeople were competing with
us convicts in stealing greens to eat. They were not only
stealing our greens, but were ripping off our vegetable
roots and outer leaves. The cooks told us, 'You can sit
at home and mutter your complaints. You don't have to
go Outside and hear what it's like. As soon as we go
Outside we don't dare let out so much as a fart. What's
more, out there everyone has to sing about how life is
so very beautiful, how people get to eat until they're
full . . .'

The millet gruel now had vegetable roots and rotten

leaves added to it, but no salt. And we were officially forbidden to buy Soy Sauce Essence. How did that work?

The Old Commissar had the power to keep the farm from applying chemical fertilizers, but he did not have the power to interfere in the enterprise of the store. Stores set up in labour reform camps did not belong to the Public Security Bureau, but rather to the commerce department. They followed a different line of authority. When commodities were scarce the commerce department's status was way above that of the Public Security Bureau. The store then became the object of everyone's fawning attention. Troop Leaders, Station Leaders, Camp Leaders, military guards all patted the horses' rumps of the attendants at the stores, begging an extra pack of cigarettes, asking that they fudge the measuring stick a little.

As a result, the Old Commissar could only forbid the convicts from buying Soy Sauce Essence – he could not prevent the store attendants from selling it. Soy Sauce Essence was a national product, not a local one. It was approved by the central government and was certainly not considered a drug. From the moment the cooks stopped using salt the business in Soy Sauce Essence at the store began to flourish.

So the Old Commissar was not able to keep the deaths of convicts within limits, and increasing numbers of people began to die. Still, for the record I want to say that he did all he could at the time. He put as much of his strength into saving us as he could.

The camps now ran into another problem. So many convicts had died that it began to be impossible to write in the official sick roll that they had all died of intestinal disorders. Citizens in society were also dying in large numbers, but when these people died their families knew why and disposed of them themselves, or the family all died together and there was no question of having someone demand an explanation. When convicts died in the labour reform camps, first it had to be reported to the management bureau of the camp. Next a form had to be handed over to the family of the convict. Even if the corpse itself could not be transferred to the family, it was necessary to say something about the cause of death. Otherwise the families of convicts would bring appeals before the Public Security Bureau, even in some cases before the Great Leader Mao Zedong. 'What did my father, husband, son, brother, daughter, mother, wife, really die of?'

Mao Zedong naturally could not admit that he had been a little confused and made the wrong decisions, that he had not listened to the advice of Peng Dehuai. He could not say that the number of people who died in 1960 from other than natural causes was enough to have fought a large-scale war.

Families would have sent someone down to investigate. Whose responsibility was it?! How did it happen?! How could so many people have died?! These were men who supported us throughout the revolutionary effort, how could they have died so easily now?

Recently I read an article that described how Chairman Mao made an investigatory trip through the south that year. He met a young girl who, to her credit, reported to him the conditions in her village. Naturally it was not the full story but it was enough and he actually started crying. Things were so bad that even the Old Man was moved. The article praised Chairman

Mao as a man full of beneficent kindness – he could even cry real tears. 'His heart was linked with the hearts of the people.' The author of the article had not done labour reform, but if he had, I guarantee he would have been one of those model, obedient intellectuals.

If families had come to investigate the cause of death of their relatives, they would have found thousands of documents with the identical wording: 'cause of death intestinal disorder'. That said all too clearly that the food and drink of the camps was unhygienic. How could *that* be reported to superiors?

So this is what happened. One day before a Central Examination Delegation was said to be coming to our camp, the Old Commissar hurriedly called together a number of male and female convicts who had studied medicine. He locked them together in a room and told them that all night long they were to revise and rewrite the causes of death of those who had died.

If those medical histories still exist, and if you have any interest in going through them, you will find that the symptoms of convicts who died were things like heart attack, congested lungs, swollen lungs, a cold turning to pneumonia, blood in the brain [stroke], plus a few intestinal and stomach disorders that were wholly unrelated to dysentery.

The Old Commissar and most of the cadres of the camp did all they could to save convicts who were dying. But from my personal experience, I believe that Chairman Mao was putting into effect his delusions of power from on high. Alone and apprehensive, he felt he was encircled by class enemies, that he had to be on guard against first this group of people, then that one; had to fight and rectify until the entire country was brought to a state of collapse. At the same time, there was a large group of cadres who were loyal to his eminence. They supported him and allowed him to continue this terrible farce.

Peasants in China have habitually accepted the authority of those who govern them. They have always tolerated their leaders' foibles. In one scene from the movie *The Last Emperor*, by the director Bertolucci, the little emperor climbs up and runs around playing after taking a shit, while a group of counsellors with tissue paper in hand chases after him trying to wipe his ass. A comparison to the emperor of the 1960s would not be inappropriate.

Death threatened all the surviving labour reform convicts. What could they do? The grain-rationing policy had been dictated from above and was a unified national fiat. The labour reform authorities had no power to add to our grain ration, and were therefore powerless to drive the god of death from the camps. Still, the labour reform cadres were born of peasant stock. Like the Old Commissar they were more familiar with peasants' proverbs than with the sayings of Marx or Lenin. From childhood they had grown accustomed to hearing their parents say, 'Even a good man fears taking three runny shits in a row.'

Right now, the convicts that Chairman Mao had given to them to oversee were unceasingly having runny shits, even if those convicts were not, strictly speaking, good men. Since they could not give the convicts additional food, they decided to try to stop up the convicts' rear-ends. If the upper hole had no more things to put in it, then stopping up the lower escape valve would have to be the solution.

A second measure was to decrease the amount of time that convicts had to work. Since convicts ate so little, let them expend less physical energy. 'Let the millet gruel work to complete efficiency' was the idea: less physical expenditure of energy plus less expelling from the rear end. On 1 May 1886, American workers demanded an eight-hour workday, but they had to go on strike and shed blood to get it. In China, labour reform convicts avoided a similar struggle – we painlessly enjoyed a substantial drop in work to far below eight hours a day.

On 25 November, the labour reform troop was again reorganized. Troops were divided into two, four, and six-hour teams, which was to say that those with the strongest bodies had to work six hours per day. In name, the troops worked for six, four, and two hours, but in fact the men would go to the field, mess around for a while, then stop work and go home again. In their spare time convicts were not, however, able to listen to music, read novels, write articles, raise their artistic consciousness or anything like that. Instead they anxiously carried out their research into expanding the variety of things humans can eat. They searched everywhere for raw material for this vital task. When the material was collected, they busied themselves with the process of preparing it: stealing charcoal, fighting over stolen charcoal, getting beaten up.

The two measures adopted by the labour reform troop noted above should have been enough to keep a lot of convicts who were on their last legs alive, albeit in a steadily worsening condition. This did not happen. As early as 14 October in the diary I noted the following: 'From the 10th, the grain ration was lowered again, this time to fifteen jin. The leaders reported that this quota would be maintained for several months, but it's hard to say.'

This concept of a grain ration per convict of fifteen jin of grain – what did it mean? 'Jin' means a market measure of jin, not a kilogram. One city or market jin was five hundred grams, so at fifteen jin per month, one had half a jin or two hundred and fifty grams per day. If there were two meals that day, that meant one hundred and twenty-five grams per meal.

The grain policy of our country included one regulation that on first sight seemed fair but in fact could only lead to gross malpractice when it was carried out. Those who were engaged in manual labour were to get fifteen jin, while office workers such as accountants, guards, supply depot personnel, etc. were to get less than fifteen jin. The thinking was that those who spent more in calories should get more to eat; those who expended less energy should get less to eat. It was precisely the latter group of people, however, that wielded the power of distributing the grain. If they had not docked the rations of those who laboured with their hands, namely us intellectual convicts, they would have been unable to survive.

In addition to the above, other people who helped themselves to some of our rations were doctors, cooks, a great crowd of free convicts, plus the Troop Leaders, Station Leaders, and Camp Leaders who directly managed the convicts. This type of person was less likely to die in China during the great famine. They all ate from the same big kitchen as we did. Assuming that grain did not flow from the kitchen to the Outside through other channels, how much of our convicts' grain did those people eat? Perhaps half.

If you calculate that in order to stay alive each of these people had to eat at least thirty-five jin of grain per month, you can estimate a number. A more empirical test confirmed it: the first time I was released from the labour reform troop I measured out one hundred and twenty-five grams of millet flour and made a sort of gruel. I stirred it down to where the consistency was identical to the millet gruel in the labour reform kitchen. The result was that, very objectively, I found that the gruel I made was more than twice as much as the gruel produced by the labour reform troop's kitchen. I believe that we were eating, at most, one hundred and twenty-five grams of millet per day. Moreover, what we ate was grain that had been weighed and ground with the husks and dirt still on it.

The two ways Troop Leaders tried to keep convicts from dying in droves had the opposite result. The forbidding of salt and consequent rise of Soy Sauce Essence was disastrous. The reorganization and new workday system merely gave convicts more time to race around outdoors looking for unhealthy things to eat. The more they ate lizards, insects, etc., the more they burst their guts and died.

This was why labour reform cadres worked so hard to search our pockets, boxes, and Numbers for illegal food. The purpose of their searches and those of camp guards in the former Soviet Union and Eastern Europe was different. Every day the Troop Leaders would line up the men and make a big search, as if they were ferreting out some great enemy. As each group of convicts came home they would first have to go through a body check. Convicts hiding cabbages or sweet potatoes or rats or toads in their clothes would often try to avoid this by charging through the gates without regard for their own safety. Struggling to get back into prison rather than struggling to get out is a phenomenon that is, again, probably unique to China.

The daily harvest resulting from the body searches was substantial. Troop Leaders were by now intimately acquainted with the extra hidden layers in convicts' clothes, so that they could point exactly to whose clothes had been doctored where.

A convict might unbutton buttons, open out upper jacket and shirt, expose the whiteness of his body, but then, without even checking the front, a Troop Leader would yell at him to turn around so he could check the back. 'Dogshitter! You think you're smarter than I am!' From along the man's spine would be peeled off a large sodden crushed leaf.

Some convicts sewed extra layers into the shoulders of their sleeves – stuffing sweet potatoes in them made them look like some kind of pretentious military officer, or some bird raising its wings. This would seldom work. A convict from the acrobatic troop could consistently pull the wool over Troop Leaders' eyes. He performed for me once and in fact it was simple, just very practised sleight of hand. But his miraculous dexterity was not something that could be learned in a short time, so every day a confiscated collection of strange things piled up in the big yard.

As a second line of defence against having convicts eat odd things and get dysentery, the Troop Leaders often held a surprise attack in the middle of the night. They would dash into our Numbers and turn everything upside down, check the bedding, the bunks, the pillows, the cases.

On 24 November, I was resting in my Number when I heard the door of the kitchen clang and experience told me that a horsecart would soon pull up by the kitchen, like the one in which I had felt around among the corpses. I raced out and prepared to steal from the cart. This time I was able to come up with real things to eat, not corpses, and I bagged several sweet potatoes.

In the middle of the next night, in one of the surprise attacks, these were 'confiscated by Dr Jin'. I remember this as though it happened yesterday. My remaining two sweet potatoes were the largest I had stolen, they were the most beautiful, adorable sweet potatoes one could imagine. My practice has always been to leave the best things to enjoy last, even books. I had carefully peeled these two sweet potatoes. After scraping away the dirt and the skin they were as sweet and glistening as the breasts of a young woman. When Dr Jin took them from under my bedding I started crying. I implored him, 'Leave them for me! Leave them for me!'

I have been arrested and sentenced five times in my life; I've been taken to the execution ground to be executed, but I never shed a tear. When those sweet potatoes were confiscated, I wept.

That night my loss of control after the incident kept me awake. Drawn up on the hard bunk, when I had calmed down a little, I felt deeply ashamed of being twenty-three years old and still capable of sobbing like a child. Near sunrise I felt that I had comprehended something, but after a minute the picture wasn't quite so clear. Many years later, I read a book on *Motivation and Human Nature*, and I think the following quotation had something to do with my enlightenment at that time:

When discussing trauma, it is easy to make the mistake of dividing people up into different components. That is to say, we talk about one whose mouth, stomach or leg has been injured. We must always remember that what has been traumatized is the entire person, not just one part of the person. Various kinds of trauma can, at the same time, threaten a person's character. They can threaten his purpose in living, his self-respect, his expression of himself, and his most basic needs.

Yes, it was not merely my stomach that had been traumatized by the loss of the sweet potatoes, but my entire person. Unable to fight back, my person, my purpose in living, my self-defence systems, my self-respect, collapsed.

'Leave them for me! Leave them for me!'

To this day I am not overly concerned that I was in labour reform for some twenty-some years and lost a normal person's enjoyment of his youth. But whenever I think of that sobbing cry, I hurt.

The focus of the body searches was that expanded range of edibles. In Soviet camps what officials were looking for were knives, scissors, files and so on, as well as any counter-revolutionary writing implements. In China, this kind of thing was not worth a glance. If a Troop Leader found something like that he would give it back to the person. 'Dogshitter. No rotten leaves, no roots, no sweet potatoes. What are these knives and scythes good for anyway?' You have to realize that convicts had been sent into the camps because they were 'class enemies', or at the very least 'contradictions among the people'. But the intuition of peasants seemed to be rather more advanced than the thought of Chairman Mao. They did not regard us as enemies at all, and certainly did not think that we would use knives and scythes to fight guards or go out and dig tunnels.

One time a Troop Leader pulled a copy of Sun Yatsen's collections from under the pillow of an intellectual, then tossed it back to him on his bunk. One couldn't eat the collected works of Sun Yatsen, and even if you could you wouldn't get runny shits. A convict nearby helped this Troop Leader deepen his political understanding, however. He told him that the book concerned the KMT's belief in the *Three Principles of the People*, and that Sun Yatsen had said that China was not suited to a communist system. Only then did the Troop Leader, still half doubting, pick up the book and take it away. A convict instructing authorities on what should be forbidden is again something that could happen only in China. I remember wondering why we needed any bosses to manage us, if we contained within our own ranks people of such acute understanding. Were we really a bunch of convicts or not?

The diary stops abruptly on 20 December. I should stop my notes there as well. Some may want to know the final results: I have to say that there is no real ending. Even long after I am gone it will be hard to close the coffin on this period and consider the debate finished. Annotating this individual record, this historical research – it is not a complete tale with a beginning and an end. Yet since I have written this as a book, it should at least have a climax, like a regular novel.

With New Year's Day of 1961 fast approaching, the diary says that the camp wanted us to guarantee that we would have a 'safe, happy New Year'. Discipline had already slackened greatly by this time. My weight was increasing and my overall health had improved. My 'materialistic attitude' to life, so criticized by others, was helping to keep me from having runny shits. My practice was to trade anything I could possibly trade for food. In addition it was now winter and there was little work to do. I mainly rested at home. My constitution had not been irrevocably damaged. I was still able to continue to write in my diary. In all, my situation was not critical.

Then, however, the labour reform camp began to talk about 'winter training'. Authorities began to demand that 'the system be tightened up'. The more material goods were lacking in the camp, the more the leaders used 'thought' to fill both people's heads and stomachs. This was described as turning the merely physical into human spirit. These indications signified to me that thought struggle among people in the labour reform camp was about to begin again in a major way.

A reader knows from this book that when intellectuals

take up the struggle against intellectuals they can be far more vicious than any peasant-born Troop Leader. A Troop Leader's rope could rip flesh from your skull and make you bleed, but it couldn't touch your soul. As a Troop Leader lashed out with his rope he always yelled, 'Had enough? Still going to do it again?' All you had to do was put on a pitiful face and say, 'I give up! I won't do it any more!' and he would stop. If by rare chance you were tied up, all you had to do was roll the whites of your eyes and plead, 'Troop Leader, have mercy on me.' He would be almost glad to loosen the rope. A Troop Leader took you as a toy to play with, something to satisfy his subconscious need to assert his own control.

The paring knife in the hands of intellectuals, on the other hand, was the weapon called 'Marxist-Leninist and Mao Zedong Thought'. This would inevitably begin by cutting away the outside manifestation of who you were, then layer by layer it would begin to scrape away your soul.

The powers of discernment of an intellectual were infinitely keener than those of a peasant-born Troop Leader. You could never pretend to an attitude and hope to get away with it. Since 1949, Chinese intellectuals had been criticized and struggled against to the point that they combined in one body a tyrannical treatment of others and a fear of being subjected to the same treatment themselves. The most suitable lifestyle for them was described by Chairman Mao: 'One must struggle every year, every month, every day.' In order to avoid being criticized and struggled against themselves, they had to pre-empt an attack and struggle against others. Yet in the course of grabbing the fire they naturally scorched themselves, and were in fact even more at risk. It went on in an unending cycle, but they couldn't stop. They couldn't break the addiction.

Intellectuals had already been struggling like this out in regular society. When they came to a place specifically created for 'reforming thought', the cruel behaviour and the reaction to it erupted at the same time so that the struggle was even more intense. Winter training was going to offer intellectual convicts an opportunity to display their struggle capabilities. What's more, I learned that the leader who would be heading our daily winter-drill training was someone who had always had his eye on me, who seemed to be able to see through me. He was an intellectual-born Troop Leader named Deng.

I was seeing corpses hauled daily out of the big yard of the labour reform camp. Men sleeping beside me were dying one after another. Letters from Mama said that she was unable to send food, and I had already been criticized for trading goods for anything edible. Based on that single criticism alone, that 'question of principle', I would surely be a target in the winter training. That is to say, all channels for acquiring food would then be cut off – the only road left to me if I stayed in the camp was the road to death. On 1 December, in the door of the infirmary, Su Ruixin said it was better on the Outside. This made a deep impression. I began to think, 'If I don't escape now, what am I waiting for?'

On 1 January 1961, on the piercingly cold morning of a New Year's Day, using the pretext of going to clean toilets in cadres' homes outside the gate of the big yard, I made my escape.

I stayed on the Outside for a full month before voluntarily surrendering myself to the camp again. I had been gone for only a few days when I became aware that this escape was a big mistake. Reality taught me a lesson. My escape became a marvellous form of self-imposed winter training.

Around 5 January, living off the grain coupons that I had traded with a free convict in exchange for some clothes. I rolled into a place called Mountain Ridge. It was in the southern part of Wei County, on the border between Ningxia and Gansu. In the afternoon I walked up to a small village of only a few houses. I selected an earthen hut set off at a little distance – I decided to approach it to ask for some water. At the door I called out a number of times without getting any response, even though I could see that there were people living inside. So I lightly pushed the door. It creaked open.

On the earthen kang straight ahead of me lay an old man and his wife; by the looks of it they were sinking fast. I had already seen many people who were breathing their last and I did not regard this as terribly unusual. I said that I didn't want to make any demands, but that I would very much appreciate a drink of water, that after drinking it I would go. The old peasant slowly raised his eyelids to look at me, then used his chin to indicate the earthen hearth. He didn't say a word.

The fire in the hearth had gone out, but the old iron pot on the stove still seemed to hold some boiled water. Wisps of steam were coming from the crack between it and the wooden cover. Next to the pot was a blue bowl that had a chip on its rim. I took up the bowl and lifted the cover, thinking to reach in and scoop some water. There was indeed hot water inside, but inside the water was something else. A dead baby.

218

I threw down the lid, spun around and left. The only part I saw clearly was a little hand, but that was enough.

I kept on towards the south after that. Surely I would find a place that had some grain for my empty stomach. Around 10 January, I reached the city of Lanzhou in Gansu Province, in the north-west. The Lanzhou train station was like a modern version of Victor Hugo's *Beggar's Kingdom*.

Here I must stop this pen and write no more. I only want to mention that I have had very little contact with Chinese peasants in my life – later when I went to work on a State Farm, the personnel engaged there were all workers drawing a salary. My writing about peasant villages is sympathetic because I was able to observe them during this time of turmoil. The large majority of beggars in the train station kingdom were peasants. I understood then that our Great Leader Chairman Mao's beneficence to convicts far exceeded his beneficence to peasants.

I experienced personally the trauma of there being absolutely nothing at all to eat, anywhere. No wonder Su Ruixin had run away once and then not tried again; no wonder that during the 'three years of natural disaster' in some regions entire villages shut themselves into their homes and starved to death. Only within an organized social structure such as a labour camp could you, with great difficulty, find enough to eat to keep you alive.

A peasant beggar I ran into in Lanzhou finally implored me to go back. 'Wherever you can get a mouthful of food is the place you should call home.' All the beggars themselves wanted to do was to go home, to eat anything that might be left there, or to die.

And so, like one of the despairing Jewish slaves led by Moses out of Egypt, thinking back regretfully to the pot left behind, my thoughts turned to the millet gruel in the labour reform camp.

One day, towards the end of January, I managed to get back to the camp. From a distance I saw its crooked gates leading to the big yard and a fierce sense of homecoming welled up inside me. My Number! My home!

It was not my one mouth, it was not my one stomach, and it was not my one life that was traumatized, but those of the entire race. The damage to a few people is perhaps not important; individuals are easily replaced. But harming the humanity of the great majority of the Chinese people, denying their self-expression, destroying their reasons for living, has lowered the human quality of all Chinese.

Although the 'natural disaster' only lasted 'three years', its severity had profound consequences. The Chinese had withstood eight years of war against the Japanese and then three years of civil war, proving that they were a resilient tribe. That they could, during the Great Cultural Revolution, prostrate themselves in unprecedented madness of worship at the feet of someone who was not unprecedentedly great and, under his banner, carry out self-flagellation in an extraordinary display of aberrant behaviour, was related to the fact that the fibre of their being had been seriously damaged several years earlier. It was damaged to the point that they lost their normal psychological balance. As one traumatized organism, the country went mad. After all these years we can still see the problems brought on by this wholesale depreciation of the character of our race.

The current 'Mao Zedong craze' and 'Return-to-the-Past craze' is only one indication of our debasement. The Chinese people have still not emerged from under the shadow of a political leader who departed long ago.

When I came back from my own variety of winter training, official winter training in the camp was reaching its peak. Exposing, criticizing and struggling were all proceeding in satisfactorily fiery-red manner. The Marxist-Leninist Thought with which intellectuals criticized each other was at such lofty and abstruse levels that barely educated cadres could scarcely understand it, let alone tell who was right.

I first went to the office to report my arrival. Outside the door I heard the cadres ridiculing intellectuals. Their ignorance of any theoretical reasoning was apparent – it was as though their heads were immersed in a dense fog. But they themselves didn't feel badly educated at all, nor did they regard intellectuals as anything special – we were to be pitied. I pushed the door open and heard the last resounding sentence, 'Motherfucker, whoever works hardest is the one who is right!'

My return interrupted their conference. The room of cadres turned to look at me. They stared hard, curious. Then they began, right in front of me, to debate how to handle my offence. The Old Commissar finally pursed his lips.

'Isn't he the one who can write poems?' he said. 'Let him be! He knows enough to have come back on his own!'

This sentence set the tone – they would not be adding years to my sentence. Although my eulogy of him had not been published under my own name it had served its purpose. Troop Leader Zheng recommended that I be sent back to my troop to be struggled against. 'He's too good at pretending to be sick and writing insincere self-examinations. Take him down a peg!' Troop Leader Deng added, 'If this next self-examination isn't a little more penetrating we'll send him into the six-hour group to work all day!'

But Troop Leader Yue then said, 'Look at this dog. All fat and sassy when he left [they had considered me fat and sassy!] and now back looking like a mangy cur. Let's lock him up for a few days in solitary first!'

Troop Leader Yue was a proper national-level cadre, while Troop Leader Zheng was merely 'doing cadre work as a substitute for being a worker'. Naturally, whatever Yue said was going to be it.

The Old Commissar asked Yue to take me over to the solitary room. On the way, Yue commented, 'How could you work now anyway? One day, and that would be the end of your measly life! You'll be able to rest a while in solitary, pull yourself together.'

The room for solitary was a separate earthen building. Its dirt floor was spread with straw made from rice stalks, but there wasn't any stove. Yue opened the door and looked around inside, then asked me if I had left behind any bedding. I told him I had, so he took me to a very large warehouse and told the guard to keep watch over me as I looked for my own belongings. I walked through this place in wide-eyed amazement. It covered three to four hundred square metres and was full of what had once been the personal property of convicts. Even in the cold it gave off a stench of mildew. Naturally most of the things belonged to dead convicts – in here somewhere, no doubt, was the golden-haired monkey jacket.

Troop Leader Yue had found me a very good place to recuperate. I slept all by myself on the rice straw, nobody squeezing me on either side. Although there was no heat, with all of my assorted clothes and bedding piled on top of me I wasn't too cold. Two meals were brought in every day, which were meant to be the same portions a regular convict was given; but since we struck up a relationship, the guard generally brought a little more. There was an iron lock on the door, but why would I have wanted to escape? I was already tired of the scenery out there and not letting me out meant I couldn't work. I could sit inside all day, immersed in my thoughts. This room for solitary was a hidden corner untouched by the fires of criticism raging through the camp. If I had known that earlier, when I escaped I would have come straight here.

Several days later, though, they sent someone in to join me and this event almost cost me my life.

When the guards dragged him in the door my first impression was that he was some kind of large dog or bear that the soldiers had caught in the mountains. Surveying him more carefully, I finally made out that he was a man, with brown sugar-beet pulp adhering to every inch of his body. The only part of the human being showing through were the whites of his eyes. When he had caught his breath and was able to open his mouth, I heard the whole story.

He was a convict from the six-hour group, which meant that he still had some strength left in his body. In the middle of the previous night he had slipped out of his Number and crept by the base of the wall along the big yard, feeling his way to a window of which he had taken note earlier. It was a back window to the kitchen. A few earthen bricks had been made ready during the day – he put these under the window to boost himself, then crawled up and inside.

Unfortunately, he ran out of energy when half of his body had been inserted into the window. Half was still sticking outside, but his muscles just would not work any more. All he could do was lie flopped over the windowsill until, because of his drawn-in stomach, he gradually slid on down into the kitchen. At a certain point he hung in the balance – head heavy, feet high in the air – before he cascaded headfirst into what was below.

Rather than sacks of grain, this turned out, much to his surprise, to be a large vat of sugar-beet pulp. This material was the by-product when they cooked sugar beets up into sugar. During the era of lowered rations, this fodder for livestock, usually pigs, was used to feed people and was considered a superior additive for things like steamed buns. The cooks would knead it into the dough, which added a touch of sweetness and also made the dough hold together. Without it, a bun would fall apart when it was cooked. Ever since the kitchen started making only gruel, this pulp was used to make special buns for the cadres. This convict had plunged headfirst into paradise and was able to indulge to his heart's desire.

Like diving into water his head went into the pool of moist pulp first; his body wallowed in it for a while until his head was able to break through to the surface. As a result he became so covered with brown sugar fibres that he did look remarkably like a brown bear.

Once in the kitchen he was not going to be satisfied with eating a little bit of sugar. He crawled out of the vat and began to stuff fistful after fistful of buns in his mouth. These were special buns that had been left on top of the stove for the cadres. Blissfully unaware of the consequences of all this, he soon found that his stomach was too full and swollen to allow much physical movement. He could forget about trying to crawl back out the window. All he could do was lie on his back on the floor with four limbs stretched out, waiting for someone to find him.

Very early the next day, before dawn, the first cook came in to start work. He opened the door to the kitchen and saw some kind of strange animal lying inside the darkness. He let out a terrified howl and almost passed out. A band of other cooks joined him, but nobody dared step inside – so many people were dying every day in the camp that rumours of angry ghosts had long been circulating among the convicts.

When the security police heard the cooks' shouts, they ordered a troop of soldiers to the spot. All these living men were terrified of dead ghosts. With guns at the ready they surrounded the building. Only when daybreak came did a stalwart, clutching his gun, finally peek through the crack in the door and discover what was inside. Since it was apparently a man, it could only be a convict. The courageous soldiers now broke down the door, marched inside and arrested him.

He told me that he was merely a worker, that he had been sent into the camp on account of stealing things to eat. Now that he was inside he was still stealing food – what to do with him? First lock him up and then decide!

We were very pleased to sit in there together. Heaven

had sent me a most agreeable partner. His body was covered with delicious pulp. As the fibres dried they formed sweet, fragrant flakes like chocolate all over him. And there were plenty of them – without even starting on his clothes, you could feast for a long time on his eyelids, hair and neck, even his feet. I could enjoy him at my convenience, just reach out and pluck ... but he himself was not allowed to move. The moment he stretched out his legs or lifted a hand, like a mud Buddha blown by the wind, the small chocolate-like flakes would drop off. They would disappear into the straw where they were impossible to retrieve.

'Is it all right for you if I just lie here like this?' he inquired. I was perhaps slightly smarter and I recommended that I first scrape off all the flakes on his body and put them in a pile on my old shirt, for our joint enjoyment. The two of us set to work at once, me first, then when I had released his arms he worked too. We peeled him off down to his toes. When he was free he stood up and did a little dance, laughing and thanking me and shouting, 'Liberated! Free!'

The next day, however, the two of us had severe diarrhoea. What came out the other end was identical in colour to brown pulp, just much runnier. Our rear-ends were like firehoses spouting an endless stream of water. When the cook came in to bring our food, he grabbed his nose and fled.

When I regained consciousness, I found I was lying in the infirmary of the labour reform camp. A dim oil-lamp was hung on the wall above my head. I watched its tiny yellow flame flicker for a long time as the supreme emptiness of impending death echoed inside me.

The infirmary had no medicine, as usual, but there

was thicker millet gruel than the ordinary, and every day they gave each patient two 'restorative pills' made of soybeans and sugar. I have never had any medicine more delicious than those pills, but they did not cure what ailed me. Whenever the doctor came to see me, he wouldn't say anything, he'd just shake his head and leave.

I probably died one night in early spring, 1961. The last thing I saw on this earth was a very round, very large moon. I don't know what the doctor wrote as the cause of the death for his records. I have the feeling that what I die of in the future will have been chosen by him back then.

I would like very much to find his notes and read them . . . but where does one go to find them?

ZHANG XIANLIANG

Grass Soup

Now one of China's major literary figures, Zhang Xianliang spent twenty-two years of his life in Mao's labour reform camps. In 1960, two years into his imprisonment, he began to keep a diary, the sole tangible record of his existence. *Grass Soup* deciphers the cryptic entries in that remarkable document, miraculously preserved from destruction and returned to its author in 1979.

'Zhang's extraordinary account tells us what it was like, in plain, wise, sometimes even humourous prose . . . it is a terrifying story . . . But it is also a glorious story, for Zhang has shown us that the human spirit can prevail, even in hell'

Independent on Sunday

'Testimony to the remarkable resilience of the human will, and a reminder of Primo Levi's precept that it is possible to keep one's humanity in the face of terrible privation'

Daily Telegraph

'Most avid and painful testimony . . . Zhang draws a map of hell that fuses the dire visions of Dante and Orwell'

Literary Review

'Extraordinary . . . worth every ounce of discomfort it may cause'

GQ

A Selected List of Titles Available from Minerva

☐	7493 9513 3	**Reservation Blues**	Sherman Alexie	£6.99
☐	7493 9931 7	**An Act of Terror**	André Brink	£7.99
☐	7493 9985 6	**Rumours of Rain**	André Brink	£6.99
☐	7493 9970 8	**Afternoon Raag**	Amit Chaudhuri	£5.99
☐	7493 9705 5	**The Name of the Rose**	Umberto Eco	£7.99
☐	7493 9760 8	**The Book of Lies**	Agota Kristof	£6.99
☐	7493 9792 6	**A River Sutra**	Gita Mehta	£5.99
☐	7493 9630 X	**A Way in the World**	V. S. Naipaul	£6.99
☐	7493 9731 4	**The Grandmother's Tale**	R. K. Narayan	£5.99
☐	7493 9604 0	**A Malgudi Omnibus**	R. K. Narayan	£6.99
☐	7493 9711 X	**The Sorrow of War**	Bao Ninh	£5.99
☐	7493 9966 X	**Lucie's Long Voyage**	Alina Reyes	£3.99
☐	7493 9035 2	**Sassafrass, Cypress and Indigo**	Notzake Shange	£6.99
☐	7493 9641 5	**Aké/Ìsarà**	Wole Soyinka	£7.99
☐	7493 9710 1	**The Makioka Sisters**	Junichirō Tanizaki	£6.99
☐	7493 9774 8	**Grass Soup**	Zhang Xianliang	£6.99
☐	7493 9852 3	**Red Sorghum**	Mo Yan	£6.99